The Official History of the
Melrose Sevens

THE OFFICIAL
HISTORY
OF THE
MELROSE
SEVENS

WALTER ALLAN

MAINSTREAM
PUBLISHING

EDINBURGH AND LONDON

First published in Great Britain in 1994 by
MAINSTREAM PUBLISHING COMPANY (EDINBURGH) LTD
7 Albany Street
Edinburgh EH1 3UG

ISBN 1 85158 660 1

A catalogue record for this book is available from
the British Library

Typeset in Palatino and Gill Sans by Litho Link Ltd,
Welshpool, Powys, Wales
Printed and bound in Great Britain by
BPC Hazell Books Ltd

CONTENTS

ACKNOWLEDGMENTS

The reasons for writing this book were purely selfish. Having spent the last ten years working in the City of London, I wanted to give myself a three-month sabbatical in which I could spend more time in the Borders. Anyone who has been brought up on either side of the Eildon Hills will know how special the place is. Secondly, my background as a reference publisher with Macmillan has made me a 'statistical junkie' on the subjects of sport and pop music, and the chance to research this book was a heaven-sent opportunity to indulge in one of my favourite pastimes. For readers under the age of 25, I am probably the last person you want to be standing next to in a pub.

I could not have written this book without the help of the Scottish rugby community. The most enjoyable aspect of writing this book was meeting some of the individuals who have helped make the history of the Melrose Sevens. The game of rugby football is truly unique, with its unwritten code of honour, sportsmanship, friendship and humour.

At the Melrose Club, I am grateful to George Bunyan, Tom Wight and the Sevens Committee for giving me complete editorial freedom to write this book. Jack Dun lent me a copy of every Melrose Sevens programme since 1933. Even as a schoolboy in the 1930s, Jack had a meticulous eye for detail, putting an asterisk against every international player who played at Melrose. A great club servant, it was only fitting that he should be President of the Club in their centenary year. Les Allan also provided me with a list of historical information and gave me some valuable advice when the book was in its first draft. My thanks are also due to Stuart Henderson, Club Secretary, for filling in some of the gaps.

At the Hawick Club, John Thorburn, Rob Welsh, Bill McLaren and Adam Robson were only too pleased to assist me with this project. In Gala, my cousin Ian Corcoran and Arthur Brown spent a most enjoyable evening with me talking about the various Gala successes.

Any thoughts of spending more time in the Borders to write this book were quickly dispelled. Interviews with Wallace Deas, Davie Edwards and Andrew Ker were fitted in between trips to London and Kent to meet up with Cameron Boyle and Ian Laughland. The return trip was via Berwick, in order that I could catch up with Ken Scotland. Finally, the only interview that took place on foot was when I walked from Kingsknowes to the Netherdale Clubrooms to meet Mr Tod.

The photographs in this volume appear courtesy of Gordon Lockie of *The Southern Reporter* whose father, like mine, was a postman in Melrose for many years. I would also like to thank the SRU's Honorary Historian and Librarian, John Davidson, who supplied the portraits of Scotland international players. All of us who have attended Melrose Sevens over the years have a favourite memory. For players, spectators, coaches and committee men, I hope these pages relive some of yours.

Finally, my thanks go to Derek Brown of Melrose RFC for writing the foreword. To date, he is the only Melrosian with a complete set of Border Sevens Medals.

Walter Allan
Galashiels
May, 1994

FOREWORD

As a very young boy I can remember Davie Sanderson, who played in the first Melrose tournament, recounting some of his memories of rugby and in particular sevens. The media of today would have had much to report, some of which would certainly receive front-page coverage.

The Greenyards has always been a second home to the Brown family. When my father was the Club Secretary, I used to go with him to the Greenyards on Saturdays and was able to gain access to the Melrose dressing-room, getting the heady smell of the embrocation used by the players, listening to the most unlikely tales told in the most lurid detail by my heroes of that era: Drummond, Crawford, the Hoggs, Johnston, Frater, Allan and Anderson. The season, as always, built up to that second Saturday in April which meant so much to the club and the Scottish rugby supporters.

Then, as an 18-year-old, I was fortunate to play in a seven with some of the characters I had so admired and I gained a coveted Melrose Medal.

We have had great pleasure and entertainment from some great club sides – Stewarts College, Melrose, Hawick, Gala, Heriots, Kelso, Rosslyn Park, Loughborough College, London Scottish, French Barbarians and Randwick – each producing some fine players.

The brainchild of Ned Haig is now played world wide, still giving tremendous enjoyment to the spectators, to the players a hard afternoon's work, often ending in bitter disappointment, but for the few, on the day, the tremendous thrill of winning.

Derek Brown
Melrose RFC

INTRODUCTION

What makes Melrose the 'Blue Riband' of the Border Sevens Circuit? Is it because of tradition, the fact that the game of sevens was invented here all those years ago by Ned Haig and his cronies, that makes the place so special? Is it the setting of the ground, nestling below the majestic drop of the Eildon Hills? Is it the meticulous planning which goes into the event which begins each year immediately after the last tournament has finished? Are you going to meet someone at Melrose whom you have not met since last year? Will you be amazed at the calibre of the guest sides who are appearing in the tournament? Is it because Melrose is a place you can take your family to enjoy a day out? Is it the proximity of the King's, the George and Abbotsford, the Bon Accord, Burt's Hotel, the Ship Inn and the Station, where you can nip in for a pint while your favourite team are taking a breather? Or is it the prospect of sampling the local delicacy – 'Der's haggis suppers' – at the end of the day? These are just some of the answers I was given when speaking to spectators who have come to Melrose over the years.

It came as something of a shock, therefore, when Douglas Morgan, the Scotland coach and former player with Stewarts/Melville FP, Scotland and the British Lions, writing in this year's programme notes, suggested:

> For how much longer will the second Saturday in April be sacrosanct as far as seven-a-side rugby is concerned? In an ever-increasing competitive world as far as 15-a-side rugby is concerned, consideration has to be given from my point of view to utilising April for 15-a-side rugby, whether for the climax of the club championship, a cup competition, premiership play-offs or even

Opposite: The Melrose President, Jack Dun, escorting the Royal Party, 1983

the Nations Championship. To my mind, if we as a nation wish to compete at the highest level in the world market-place, we must look to playing 15-a-side rugby in conditions which are more conducive to playing better rugby.

This begs the question, who are the most important people involved in rugby union? The answer has got to be the players. As commercialisation and sponsorship have come into the game, the season has been extended so that players are now playing competitive rugby from the beginning of September and, with end-of-season tours now a regular occurrence, some players are getting hardly any break at all. An alarming trend over the past few seasons has been the number of international players who have retired at a

Keith Robertson, who has entertained the Greenyards faithful for almost 20 years

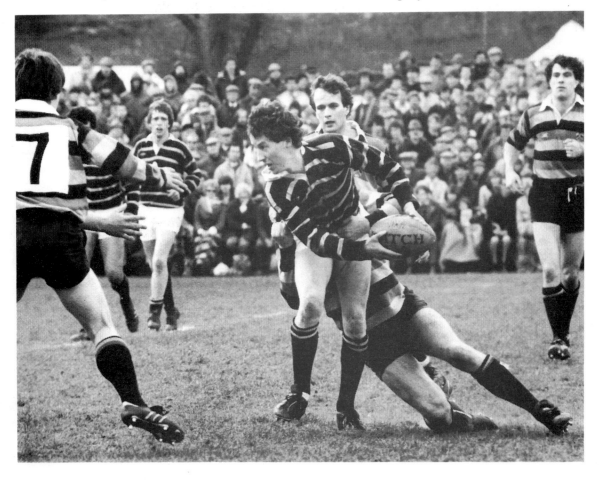

relatively young age. What they are saying is that they have had enough.

Overseas tours are an invaluable part of a player's education, building up team spirit and fitness and all the rest, but surely it would make more sense to have the tours at the beginning instead of the end of an arduous season.

There is tremendous pressure placed on the players of today, especially those whose clubs are involved in promotion and relegation, and the end-of-season Border Sevens tournaments provide players with some relief and enjoyment, away from the rigours of national league rugby. Andrew Ker believes that seven-a-side rugby should be about entertainment, and you just needed to look at their faces when they scored to see how much enjoyment the likes of Jim Renwick, Keith Robertson, Arthur Brown and the like derived from playing sevens.

Hawick still hold the record at Melrose for the highest number of wins, with 29. However, Hawick have not recorded a victory at Melrose since 1967. I wonder how many caps Colin Deans and Jim Renwick would swap for a Melrose Medal.

Who are the best seven ever to have played at Melrose? It is impossible to compare players from different eras but some of the following teams might spring to mind.

In the 1920s, Hawick were Queen of the Borders, winning five titles during that period with A. Bowie becoming the first player to win 50 Border Sevens medals.

Heriots had a marvellous side during the 1930s and won three titles in a row between 1938 and 1940 with Sam Oxley, probably one of the first black players to be seen in the Borders.

Melrose were the great team of the immediate post-war years with Charlie Drummond, Alastair Frater and the Hogg brothers going through their repertoire of tricks.

Heriots and Stewarts colleges were the most consistent city challengers during the 1950s, with Heriots winning in 1954, 1957 and 1958. Ernie Anderson and the Sharp brothers kept the crowd on their feet, and the Stewarts scrum-half must be one of the best players to have played at Melrose and not won a winners' medal.

The Cambridge University side of 1960 were regarded by some as the best team to have played at Melrose. With five Scotsmen in their ranks, they were certainly one of the most popular.

Campese, 1990

London Scottish were the most consistent of the teams during the early 1960s, winning both Melrose and Middlesex during the same season.

The composite Hawick Seven of 1966 and 1967 won ten Border tournaments in a row, a feat which is unlikely to be equalled.

Gala's best period was between 1970 and 1972 when the 'magnificent seven' achieved three in a row, with Duncan Paterson joining the élite club of players with 50 Border Sevens medals. The rest of the decade produced some of the most competitive ties ever seen at Melrose with a different team winning every year between 1973 and 1979.

The 1980s were dominated by Kelso and between 1978 and 1993 they appeared in 13 finals. J.J.'s try against Wasps in the semi-final in 1986 would certainly be a contender for the best try ever seen at Melrose.

During the 1990s, Gala proved that it was possible to win at Melrose playing five ties and to beat the seeded guest sides. My own favourite side from the 1990s were Randwick. I would have happily paid to watch Campese and Co. go through their training routine. The most exciting tie ever seen at the Greenyards must have been the Randwick v. Melrose semi-final in 1990 in which Keith Robertson, at the age of 35, played against David Campese.

The future for Melrose Rugby Club looks extremely bright. They have just won the National League title and the Border League. The club have just signed a new six-figure sponsorship deal with United Distillers and the tournament will still be known as the Bell's Melrose Sevens. Jim Telfer, who has recently taken up the appointment of Director of Coaching at the SRU, has left a wealth of experience with the club coaches. The Crichton Cup celebrated its 75th anniversary this year. Another generation of players for Melrose Colts.

Next year will see the 105th Melrose Sevens take place. A note for your diary: Saturday, 8 April 1995.

THE ORIGINS AND HISTORY OF SEVENS RUGBY

The Melrose Sevens

The picturesque Border Abbey town of Melrose attracts tourists and visitors from all over the world during the summer months, and the remains of the twelfth-century Cistercian Abbey are a notable Border landmark. However, of greater significance to the town is the second Saturday in April when 12,000 spectators come and watch what is now regarded as the 'Blue Riband' of the Border Spring Sevens Circuit.

The game of rugby football is the most popular pastime for the young men of the Scottish Southern Uplands and the skills, traditions and folklore have been handed down from one generation to the next.

For the past century, the major industry of the Scottish Borders has been textiles and it is believed that rugby was first played in Scotland in the 1870s when Yorkshire woollen manufacturers set up factories in nearby Hawick and Galashiels, with several Yorkshire families settling in the area after moving north with their employers.

A popular sport around this time was 'handba', which was played in the neighbouring towns and villages and is still played today. The game is said to have its barbaric origins in the Middle Ages when, after an Anglo/Scottish border skirmish, the heads of fallen English soldiers would be cut off and thrown, for a bit of sport, from hand to hand or even kicked.

The rules of the game were quite simple. The contest was between two teams, the uppies and the doonies. The uppies would live in one half of the town or village and the doonies in the other. The object of the game was to carry the ball into enemy territory, which would either be over a wall, field or stream, and the ball would be hailed, i.e. thrown over the gain line. In some towns and villages the balls would be donated by couples who were married in that parish during the year. The groom would kick the ball off and a huge ruck or scrum would emerge until someone collected the ball and ran with it towards the other team's boundary. The game would sometimes last all day, depending on how many games were played, and the winning team were the ones who had 'hailed' the most balls during the day. It is only within the last ten years that this activity has stopped because no insurance company would pay out on damages to limbs or property. However, Craig Chalmers was given permission for his marriage ball to be kicked off in Melrose during his recent wedding.

Against this background, it is little wonder that the Borders was a fertile nursery for this game of rugby football. Among the first clubs to be started was that of Gala. In the autumn of 1873 two Englishmen from Yorkshire named Hudson and Fraser, the former in the textile industry, the latter an engineer in Galashiels, proposed to form a football club. They gathered around them the sons of a number of manufacturers and others who had learned the game at school, and it was not long before the necessary materials for starting a club were forthcoming. Other recruits were obtained from the neighbouring towns of Selkirk and Melrose and there was no scarcity of players even for the 20-a-side game which then prevailed. The first game was a memorable affair and was played on what is now the Gala Public Park. There were no goalposts in the park so whenever a game was played the posts had to be carried out by the players and erected before the game could commence. The first posts were provided by Mr John Hall, of J. & T. Hall Builders, who was an enthusiastic member of the club. The crossbar was hoisted to the required height by means of pulleys. The costume of the players was somewhat amusing. There were no shorts – each player wore blue trousers, a blue jersey and a red pirnie (or cap). The pirnies were discarded after the first two or three matches as more were scattered over the field than remained on the owners' heads. A forerunner to the scrum cap no doubt.

A considerable contingent of the players belonged to Melrose and after the club had been in existence for a year or so the players from the Abbey town became more numerous and asserted their voices in the management of the club's affairs. The Melrose players considered that, as they had nearly as many players in the team as

Gala, the club should be a combined one and bear the name of Melrose as well and that half of the home matches should be played at Galashiels and the other half at Melrose. This was resented by the Gala section who had quite enough players of their own to maintain a club and, after a long wrangle, the outcome was that the Melrose men went off and formed a club of their own. By an amazing coincidence, a set of goalposts disappeared overnight and, just as mysteriously, a new set of posts had arrived at the Greenyards. (The Melrose ground takes its name from the 'Green Yairds' where the medieval Cistercian monks had their individual plots of land.)

Tradition has it, for there are no official records of the period, that in 1883 Melrose Football Club were trying to find a way to raise money to help club finances when the suggestion of a football tournament was put forward by the legendary Ned Haig. Ironically, one of the reasons why Melrose could have been in such financial plight was an incident which happened at the match between Melrose and Gala at the Greenyards in the 1882–83 season.

The games between these Border rivals always created the liveliest interest and, as the team was always accompanied to these and some of their other matches with the town band, there was always a great following of supporters. For reasons now unclear, on the Tuesday before the match when the placards making the announcement were posted on the walls, the Gala supporters were surprised to observe that the charge for admission had been raised to sixpence. As the charge for admission had hitherto only been threepence, the increased tariff was regarded as a gross imposition. On the day before the match, however, the town bellman paraded the streets and made an announcement advising the Gala followers that if the charge of sixpence was insisted upon by Melrose they were to remain outside the field and boycott the match. Saturday came and a special train was required to convey the large following of Gala supporters to Melrose, but on arriving at the gate it was found that the increased charge was to be enforced. This was sufficient for the Gala contingent, most of whom adopted the advice given and remained outside, although a few gave way and paid their 'tanner' under protest. Seeing they were going to have the worst of the bargain, the Melrose Committee decided to revert to the old charge and just before the match an announcement was made to this effect. Hundreds of Gala supporters rushed to the gate and the police and stewards were carried away by the mass, and most of the visitors were able to enter the ground without paying. It was as bad on the pitch for Melrose as well. During the game, Scarborough scored a try for Gala which the Rose players disputed and they promptly left the pitch. They returned ten minutes later and were jubilant when they thought they had scored. The referee and the Gala umpire disallowed the goal and the Melrose players left the field in a huff for the second time.

Ned Haig

Ned Haig was born in the town of Jedburgh on 7 December 1858 and came to neighbouring Melrose as a teenager, presumably to find employment. He was taken on in the town by local butcher Davie Sanderson, with whom he would link at quarter-back to become one of the first Melrose Sevens winners.

He made his début for Melrose in 1880 at the age of 22, was a regular member of the 1st XV and made several representative appearances for the South of Scotland.

When his playing career ended, he continued to take an active part in the club and was on the Committee for several seasons. In addition, he participated in cricket, curling and golf. He had a long life for someone born in the Victorian era and died on 28 March 1939 at the ripe old age of 80.

In an article, probably written just after the turn of the century, in *An old Melrose Player's Recollections*, Haig recalls:

> Want of money made us rack our brains as to what was to be done to keep the club from going to the wall, and the idea struck us that a football tournament might prove attractive but as it was hopeless to think of having several games in one afternoon with 15 players on each side, the teams were reduced to seven men.

Opposite: Ned Haig, the originator of seven-a-side rugby

According to Dr John Gilbert, author of *Melrose Rugby Football Club 1877–1977*, and Jack Dun, President of the Club during their centenary sevens:

Haig's contribution according to that statement by himself was the idea of a football tournament. The wording suggests that the reduction to seven players per side was the outcome of discussion among some or probably all of the club's officials of the mechanics of running such a tournament. It is not possible to say whether a football tournament with an athletic event, or an athletics event with a football tournament was the original idea.

Whatever the truth of the matter may be, generations of spectators and players have been grateful that the Melrose Sports were started and included a football tournament. Originally, the seven players comprised a full-back, two quarter-backs and four forwards, but with the development of the passing game, the forwards were reduced to three and an extra half-back played.

Initially, the programme contained foot races, drop-kicks, dribbling races and place-kicking. The football competition, however, was the main attraction and a cup was presented for it by 'the ladies of Melrose'. A drop-kick competition had featured at Highfield Academy Sports, but never had the idea of a football competition been mooted.

The Border Advertiser from Wednesday, 2 May 1883, published the following report from the first ever Melrose Sevens:

Under the auspices of the above club the Sports were held in the Greenyards field on Saturday. The event began at 12.30 and concluded at 7.15. The day was not very favourable, being very cold during the forepart and wet long before the close.

By the time the competition had started an enormous crowd of spectators had gathered, special trains having been run from Galashiels and Hawick and about 1,600 tickets being taken at Melrose during the day. From the former place alone there were 862 persons booked, of whom 509 came by special train and the other 353 by ordinary train. Despite the crowd and open character of the field, there was no attempt on this occasion to force entry without payment, the ground being kept by a large staff of County Police under Mr Porter. As football has been the popular game of the season in the district, perhaps its nature corresponds with the spirit of the hardy Borderers. The competition had been looked forward to with great interest as most of the clubs of the district were expected to compete for the prize – a silver cup presented by the ladies of Melrose.

Opposite: Ned Haig's gravestone nestling beneath the Eildon Hills

EDWARD "NED" HAIG
BORN AT JEDBURGH
7TH DECR 1858
DIED AT MELROSE
29TH MARCH 1939.

ERECTED BY
THE BORDER RUGBY CLUBS
IN MEMORY
OF THE ORIGINATOR
OF SEVEN-A-SIDE RUGBY.

The excitement during the game was thus great and that portion of the spectators belonging to the various townships did all it could to encourage its club or clubs. Specially was this the case on the part of the Galashiels people who leaped the barrier on several occasions at critical points of play by their club and mixed among the players. To their credit be it said, yet, no portion of spectators, however warm their feelings, interfered with any of the clubs. The competition was played under rugby rules – 15 minutes' play being allowed to each heat, and seven members of each club competing. The regulations were that in the first heat should two clubs tie, they would both be allowed to play in the second, should two clubs tie in the second round of the competition, they shall play on until one scores, when that one shall be declared the winner of the heat.

Melrose and Gala were left to decide the result of the final. The ground by this time was soft and slippery owing to the rain and the Gala team were pretty well knocked-up after a tough contest with St Cuthberts. After a short interval, however, they were forced to begin again or run the risk of being disqualified. The Melrose team had a long rest and the two clubs they had played previously were both light and they were therefore much fresher than their opponents. The interest of the spectators in the proceedings now increased and the result was contemplated with considerable curiosity, as it was known that keen rivalry existed between the two clubs, both having denied defeat in the last match played between them.

They played for 15 minutes, a fast and rough game but, as nothing was scored, it was agreed by the captains to play another quarter of an hour. After ten minutes play, Melrose obtained a try and left the field without either trying to kick their goal or finishing the game, claiming the cup; but their title to do so was challenged by Gala on the grounds that the game had not been finished. The proceedings were then brought to an abrupt conclusion and the spectators left the ground amid much noise and confusion. It is said the referee decided the tie in favour of Melrose but that they should have played the quarter of an hour before they were entitled to claim the cup. The Galashiels supporters were warm in their declaration that their townsmen had hardly got justice, and the opinion generally expressed was that the final should have been postponed to another day, in order to give both clubs fair play.

The Border Advertiser was the forerunner to *The Border Telegraph*, a weekly paper published in Galashiels. Even in those days rugby scribes were biased in favour of the palemerks!

Finalists

Melrose: J. Simson, D. Sanderson, N. Haig, J. Riddell, T. Riddell, G. Mercer and J. Tacket.

Gala: A.J. Sanderson, J. Hewat, W. Rae, W. Wear, T. Oliver, J. Ward and T. Smith.

John Hart, writing in *The Southern Journal* for 1957, describes the first Melrose Sevens thus:

For their first Sports, the Melrose Seven wore white jerseys, each adorned with a hand-sewn badge on the pocket. Their jerseys were presented by the ladies of Melrose, who took a great interest in the young side. There was one referee and two umpires, one on each side of the scrum and no touch running. An umpire would raise his flag for an infringement and the referee might then blow his whistle. This made for fewer penalties. A touchdown counted against the defending side.

J. Simson, D. Sanderson, N. Haig, J. Riddell, T. Riddell, G. Mercer and J. Tacket formed the Melrose team. J. Simson, the full-back, had a safe pair of hands and a fair turn of speed. He linked well with his quarter-backs and fully realised the basic principle of sevens, i.e. ball possession. D. Sanderson and N. Haig were outstanding quarter-backs who combined with an understanding which frequently bewildered their opponents. Sanderson was not a tall man but strong and quick in his acceleration. He side-stepped and swerved most elusively. Haig was taller and never gave up until the final whistle. J. Riddell, a forward, excelled in defence and attack. T. Riddell, another forward, fast and powerful, blended well with his team mates. G. Mercer was also a forward but sufficiently versatile to be able to play behind the scrum with distinction. J. Tacket was a hard-working forward who was famed, not only for his goal-kicking, but also for his first-rate dribbling. Training was on the high road near Leaderfoot Bridge. Little imagination is needed to picture their discussions on the style and pattern of play, on the importance of ball possession and about the difference between seven-a-side and 15-a-side tactics.

What's in a Medal?

Until recently, it has been assumed that the winners of the Melrose Sevens of 1883 had received the Ladies Cup only and that medals were first introduced two years later, in 1885. Strict rules about professionalism and the amount of money that could be spent on prizes were solemnly adhered to or you received a rap from the Scottish Rugby Union.

In 1990 the Melrose Club were presented with an 1885 medal which belonged to the legendary Davie Sanderson, scorer of the winning try in 1883, and employer of Ned Haig. Astonishingly, the donor was Sanderson's daughter, Mrs Cathy Wheelans. In memory of her father, she donated the Sanderson Salver for annual presentation to the runners-up at Melrose Sevens.

Davie Sanderson, as captain, kept the original Ladies Cup and it was many years before he passed the trophy back to Honorary Secretary Bob Brown, which begs the question: was the 1883 tournament intended to be a one-off event?

In 1992, Ronald Watson, a native of Melrose, produced a winner's medal for the first Melrose Sports, dated 1883, which

The Ladies Cup, 1883

belonged to his mother. She was the granddaughter of John Tacket, the famous goal-kicker and dribbler of the first Melrose Seven. Tacket's medal was in its original box and the inscription on the medal reads: 'Presented to J. Tacket – one of the winning seven for the Ladies Cup. Played at Melrose April 28th 1883'. How could the club find another one to authenticate it? Les Allan takes up the story: 'A few years ago a Mr Simson from America visited the club and claimed to be the grandson of John Simson, who was the winger in that first seven, and that he had back home a rugby memento belonging to his grandfather. Was it the medal from 1883 and did it have the same inscription on it as Jack Tacket's? Honorary Secretary Stuart Henderson managed to contact Simson and he was able to verify that what he had was indeed an original medal and the inscription on it was the same as Tacket's.'

To date, only two of the original winning medals have been recovered. If any reader has any information about these other five medals, the Committee of Melrose RFC would love to hear from you. Meanwhile, courtesy of Ron Watson, Tacket's medal was on loan and on display in the Ned Haig Bar at the Greenyards clubrooms.

The Growth of Sevens in Scotland

Following the commercial success of the Melrose Sevens in 1883, other Border clubs were quick to follow suit, eager to swell their coffers. In 1884 Galashiels FC introduced a seven-a-side tournament and, like Melrose, won their own tournament in the first year. Hawick Sports were started in 1885 and, when Jedforest hosted their first tournament in 1894, Hawick won the first Jedburgh Sports. In 1908 Langholm followed suit, and the Border Spring Circuit of five sevens on successive Saturdays began.

By this time invitations to play in the Border Sevens were not confined to Border clubs. St George, popularly known as the Dragons, appeared at Melrose as early as 1887 with Heriots, Stewarts and Watsonians quickly following suit.

The next development was for tournaments to be staged outside the Borders. Four Border clubs were invited to the inaugural St George's tournament, which Melrose won in 1909 and 1910. Edinburgh Academicals, Edinburgh University, Athenians, Royal High School and Glasgow High School started sending sevens down to Melrose and the popularity of the sport was growing in both Edinburgh and Glasgow.

After the Great War there was further expansion locally and nationally. Selkirk Sports began in 1919, Kelso in 1920, with junior sides Earlston and Peebles joining the bandwagon in 1923. The new tournaments took place at the beginning of the season in September and there were now eight Border Sevens.

In 1920 the Royal High School ran a tournament in the Scottish Rugby Union's field in Edinburgh to aid a War Memorial Fund. This objective prompted Edinburgh Institution, in 1921, and Kelvinside Academicals, in 1922, to stage their own tournaments. The

A Melrose cap, as worn by the captain of the club. This one belonged to J. Mars, captain, 1894–95

Edinburgh Borderers began their tournament at Granton in 1922 and the following year several Edinburgh clubs met and decided to stage a tournament on 7 April in aid of an Edinburgh charity. This began the Infirmary Sevens. Seven-a-side rugby is now played all over Scotland, and in 1973 the first international tournament was held at Murrayfield 90 years after the historic first tournament in Melrose. The winners were England.

In the Home Unions

With Tynedale and Carlisle receiving invitations to the early Border Sports, it was not surprising that seven-a-side competitions should flourish in the north of England. In 1921 a Melrose side lost to Selkirk in the final of the Percy Park Sports at North Shields. Rockcliffe and Northumberland both received permission to hold sevens in 1922, as did Carlisle the following year. Kendal tried to introduce a nine-a-side competition, but the English Rugby Union only gave permission for seven-a-side. In 1926 Halifax attempted to stage a tournament in July, but the application was turned down. The best known of the English Sevens was given the green light on 26 August 1925 when Middlesex County were granted permission to stage a sevens competition and the first was held at Twickenham on 24 April 1926. Not surprisingly, it was a Scot, Mr J.A. Russell Cargill, whose enthusiasm for the game stirred the interest of rugby followers in the Home Counties, and so started the now famous Middlesex Sevens. Melrose were invited to participate in the Middlesex Sevens in 1952 but the Committee of that time turned the invitation down as the tournament clashed with the Langholm Sevens and they didn't want to offend Langholm. All the players were disappointed and Charlie Drummond, as captain, was so incensed he 'fixed it' to get the invitation revived again. This was achieved, but to everybody's consternation the Committee turned it down once more. The success of this tournament encouraged other clubs in the Midlands and the south of England to hold similar tournaments. In recent years, however, seven-a-side rugby in

England has suffered from the extension of the 15-a-side season.

In Wales, seven-a-side rugby is widely played today, but it was not until 1950 that the Old Penantians Sevens took place. It received recognition with the introduction of the Snelling Seven-a-side Competition in 1954, and in 1966 the Welsh Rugby Union National Sevens were started.

The first ever sevens played in Ireland were the *Evening Mail* Sevens played in Dublin in 1926, but the Old Belvedere Sevens remains the élite tournament of the All Ireland Circuit. The first winners, in 1971, were Loughborough Students.

The Rest of the World

The spread of sevens rugby

Following the success of the Scotland Centenary Sevens, the World Cup Sevens returned to Murrayfield 20 years later, when no fewer than 24 nations from five continents took part in a competition for the Melrose Cup in honour of the town where the first seven-a-side tournament took place. The following countries took part:

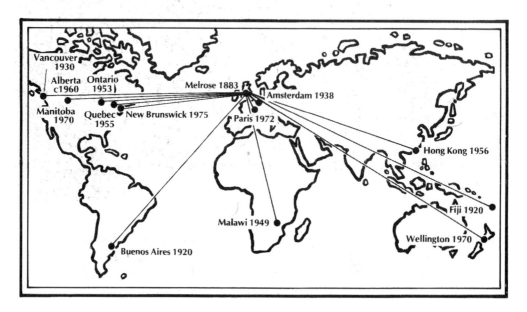

Argentina – Seven-a-side rugby is extremely popular in this country and the Buenos Aires Sevens (1921) is the oldest tournament outside Scotland, but most of the 14 provincial unions also hold these end-of-year competitions.

Australia – The first domestic tournament in Australia took place in 1971, the Kioma Sevens in New South Wales. Canberra is the newest and most prestigious of the Australian sevens. However, rugby union is still behind rugby league and Australian Rules in the popularity stakes.

A family affair: Melrose President Mac Brown watches his mother, Peggy, present the Ladies Cup to the Randwick Skipper

Canada – The game has been played in British Columbia for many years, with occasional tournaments taking place in the 1930s. The Robert Spray Cup was first played for in 1953, and in 1975 the Vancouver Club decided to host a Middlesex-style tournament.

England – Although Percy Park can rightly claim to have the oldest sevens south of the border, the Middlesex Sevens is England's most prestigious tournament. It gives junior clubs an opportunity to take on the top London clubs.

Fiji – The first domestic tournament did not take place until 1977, with the Maarist Sevens, but this extraordinary Polynesian nation has dominated international events in recent years. They actually prefer sevens to 15s. Natural ball handlers, they now play sevens all the year round.

The French legend Serge Blanco stopped in his tracks

France – The Paris University Club were the first side in France to organise a sevens tournament, in 1959. Two years later, London Scottish were the first overseas winners. However, despite French flair in the 15s, the development of seven-a-side rugby in France has been curtailed because of the overwhelming significance of the French Championship.

Holland – Rugby football in the Netherlands is a very poor second to soccer but the international side still play with the famous orange jersey. The game is gaining popularity in the universities, and the first sevens tournament took place in the Hook of Holland. In recent years, the Heineken Sevens have become very popular.

Hong Kong – The two original Hong Kong tournaments were the Bill Riach Sevens held by the Royal Hong Kong Police Rugby Club and started in 1968, and the Blarney Stone Sevens held by Hong Kong FC. However, following the success of the Scotland Centenary Sevens held at Murrayfield in 1973, a group of Hong Kong expatriates created a truly international annual sevens competition and, with the sponsorship of Cathay Pacific and Hong Kong Bank, it rapidly became the tournament where the best players in the world take part.

Ireland – The Irish have supplied some outstanding sevens players over the years. They supplied a star-studded Co-optimist side in the 1950s with the likes of Tony O'Reilly, Karl Mullen and Andy Mulligan. Mike Gibson was the player of the tournament in the 1973 Centenary Sevens, and Karl Mullen returned to Melrose in 1991 with his successful Irish Wolfhounds.

Italy – The Algida side from Rome were the first organisers of a seven-a-side tournament in Italy in 1974, and in 1979 Carwyn James, the then Dorigo coach, persuaded his club to launch a sevens tournament. London Scottish, captained by Mike Biggar, won the first event in 1980.

Japan – Sevens is not popular in Japan and until 1992 the only two domestic tournaments of any note were the ones held at Yokohama and Kohe. Exorbitant land prices prevent the development of new pitches, but there are 180,000 players playing for 3,000 clubs and these are centred around the universities and the large corporations.

Korea – One of the few rugby-playing Asian nations where the sport was not developed as an expatriate game. They only have one domestic competition, the National Championship which was started in 1962, but the Koreans are more geared to the 15-a-side game, having 80 clubs.

Latvia – The surprise package of the World Cup Sevens. They obtained their passage to the finals by beating Russia 12–10 at the Moscow Sevens to clinch a qualifying place at Murrayfield, but the game of rugby is only 24 years old in this new country.

Namibia – The first overseas visitors to Namibia were the British Lions in 1955, but its oldest sevens tournament, run by Windhoek United RFC, is only seven years old. With only 1,250 senior players to choose from, the prospect of expanding seven-a-side rugby is limited.

Kelso v. Randwick, 1990

New Zealand – Although rugby union is the national game of New

Zealand, it was not until the Middlesex County RFU donated a cup to celebrate their centenary in 1949 that the Kiwis competed at seven-a-side. By 1978 the national Middlesex Cup competition had run out of steam and, since then, under Bill Freeman, they have concentrated on prestigious international events.

Romania – The first sevens tournament to be held in Romania took place in Bucharest in 1985, the year before Romania made their international début at the New South Wales World Sevens in Sydney. In 1992, after the revolution, Romania played in the Hong Kong Sevens, where they won the Bowl final.

Scotland – Home of rugby sevens. The first game of rugby took place in Scotland in 1858 when Merchiston Castle took on Edinburgh Academy. The Scottish Rugby Union was formed in 1875. Eight years later Ned Haig and his colleagues discussed the abbreviated system, and the game is now played all over the world.

South Africa – Years in the political wilderness have robbed two generations of South Africans of the opportunity to compete in international sevens. The first domestic tournament did not take place until the Ford Sevens were held in Pretoria in 1973 and, for a country steeped in rugby-playing tradition, it was not until 1993 that they made their international début in the Hong Kong Sevens.

Spain – Rugby was first played in Spain in the Basque country, but it faces an uphill struggle to compete for popularity with soccer and Barcelona FC. The first sevens tournament was held at Madrid University in 1955 and, in recent years, the Spanish national side have recorded impressive wins over England and Hong Kong.

Taiwan – If the Taiwanese feel that they are missing out on something, they send their fellow countrymen out on a fact-finding mission. In rugby, it is no different. The Taiwanese national squad were sent to New Zealand, and it would be no surprise if they emerged as Asia's strongest rugby nation. The first sevens tournament was held in Taipei Town in 1946.

*The Cougars v.
Jedforest*

USA – The USA can boast of a record that no other country will achieve. They are the reigning Olympic Champions in rugby. However, rugby has not featured at the Olympics since 1924. Sevens in the States started on a localities basis, with the East Coast providing most of the clubs. The New York Sevens started back in 1959, when it was won by MIT. Since 1985, sponsorship from Michelin has given the USA RFC a national-club sevens championship played in Washington DC.

Wales – For a country that has produced players of the calibre of Gerald Davies, Davie Watkins and Jonathan Davies, the Welsh public have shown a surprising indifference to the seven-a-side game. For a number of years, the Snelling Sevens were a great success and the tournament grew in size until the late 1960s, but it eventually suffered from the lack of an adequate qualifying system.

Western Samoa – The country became a British protectorate in 1914 under the administration of New Zealand, and within six years the first sevens were being played at Maarist School. The famous war dance Marluulu, performed by Samoan warriors Manu Samoa, has struck fear into many opposing teams and they are arguably one of the most talented seven-a-side playing nations in the world.

According to Marcel Martin, Chairman of the Rugby World Cup:

The Rugby World Cup Sevens represents more than the fruition of Haig's wildest dreams. It constitutes another piece in the ongoing Rugby World Cup plan, building a platform for the development of the game of rugby union worldwide. The sevens were seen in more than 60 countries around the world, and the surplus from the tournament will be ploughed back into the Rugby World Cup programme. Commercially, the RWC Sevens represents an additional segment which has been successfully woven into the four-year RWC cycle, creating a seamless upward progression from the success of RWC in 1991. With this infrastructure now firmly in place, we have a basis for building the long-term relationships with sponsors and broadcasters which will aid the ongoing success of the event and, with it, the game internationally.

By making a few changes in the laws and regulations on a spring Saturday in the Scottish Borders in 1883, who would have believed that just over a century later, the brainchild of Ned Haig would have become an international, multi-million pound industry?

THE EARLY DAYS 1884–1915

A try by Davie Sanderson in extra time had given Melrose victory in the first ever tournament, but the following year Gala gained revenge in the final, defeating Melrose. An account from *The Border Advertiser*, Wednesday 23 April, describes the occasion:

FINAL — MELROSE V. GALA

A. Sanderson kicked the ball off for Gala and the Gala forwards were on to it before it could be returned. The play at the beginning was confined to the Melrose ground and A. Sanderson got a grand run, passing all his opponents, but he was eventually held. A short time after, however, Scarborough got hold of the leather about the Melrose 25, he passed all his opponents in grand style, not one of them being able to hold him, and scored the winning points for the Gala lads amidst deafening cheers. He took the place at goal and the ball just went past the side of the post. The ball being kicked-off at the 25, the game became very fast. The Melrose forwards played splendidly but A. Sanderson proved himself equal to the occasion, stopping their pushes in fine style.

Scarborough again had a grand run, being held a few yards from the Melrose goal-line before he was brought down. Gradually, however, the Melrose forwards got the ball down the field and from a hard kick by Riddell, it went into touch a few feet from the Gala line. The result was watched with great eagerness by the spectators. The ball was thrown in by a Gala player but it was kicked into touch again. It was now Melrose ball and it was thrown far out to D. Sanderson, Scarborough, however, was on the alert, bringing him to the ground. Time was shortly afterwards called and the Gala team left the field victorious. They were greeted with ringing cheers and some of them were carried shoulder high. For the winning team, Scarborough proved to be the swiftest man on the field. He

A. Haig and D. Sanderson with the Ladies Cup, 1883

secured a try each time his team played and his kicking was also splendid. A.J. Sanderson was the right man in the right place for tackling and all the others played their parts well. The band, on reaching the Galashiels station accompanied by a large crowd, played 'The Conquering Hero' from there to the market place, where the crowd dispersed with three cheers for the winners.

The winning Gala team were T.L. Scarborough, A.J. Sanderson, H. Roberts, A.T. Clay, T. Oliver, J. Ward and J. Hewitt.

Remarkably, the Melrose club still have a direct link with the 1885 tournament because not only did Melrose win but almost a century later Cathy Whelans, daughter of Davie Sanderson, presented to the club her father's winning medal.

In the 1886 tournament, one of the semi-finals between Hawick and Melrose remained unfinished on the Saturday and was played on the Wednesday night and, after a fast and hard game lasting 57 minutes, the game ended with a win for the home team by two tries to one. Tynedale, the first English club to win at Melrose, beat the host side in the final by two tries to nil.

By 1887, the annual Amateur Athletic Sports Meeting at Melrose was a major sporting event and a crowd of over 4,000 spectators witnessed the various sporting fixtures. The day was extremely favourable and a grandstand erected on the field was well filled by many of the gentry of the district. Special trains brought large numbers of people from Gala, Hawick and other areas in the district. Once again the semi-finals were not contested on the Saturday. Hawick and Wilton faced Gala Thistle with a man short, with Rodger having been hurt during Saturday's play. A quarter of an hour was played with no result and ends were changed, which favoured the Braw Lads who won by a try scored by Burrell who got in at the posts. Gala Thistle then met Hawick in the final. After a gruelling semi-final tie, the Thistle were given little time for recovery but after 20 minutes in the final there was no scoring. Ends were changed, but it took a further 15 minutes to separate the teams when Burnett touched down for the Greens.

In 1888, Roxburghshire Police Force had to interfere and stop several fights which occurred on the way between the railway station and the ground. Those who actually managed to watch the

The first Melrose Seven – winners, 1883

rugby saw Hawick and Wilton defeat Gala by 8–3 in the final.

A crowd of 5,000 visited Melrose in 1889, and *The Border Advertiser*, 24 April 1889, describes the final between Hawick and Melrose:

The home team kicked-off into touch at the visitors' 25, the latter returned the leather to neutral grass and the Melrose pack dribbled down. Burnett kicked back to their territory and Rodd had a short run followed by some passing by his comrades, which gained them some advantage. Bunyan and Brown toed the ball back to midfield. At this stage a fight emerged amongst the spectators who invaded the ground so much that play had to be stopped, and a hard chain was formed to keep the intruders back. On resuming, Scott had a run but Morrison brought him down. Wilson dribbled towards the line but Reid relieved with a big punt and Turnbull kicked to the half-way line. Again Morrison had to stop Scott and then Bunyan, by a run, took the venue of play to the Greens' 25. Hawick reversed matters and they were dangerously near the Melrose posts when the half-time whistle blew. On crossing over, Wilson charged over Morrison's return and play opened at the Melrosian 25. Bunyan made headway but passing by Wilson made them lose ground and Hogg rushed off and nearly scored, Sanderson having to trot the ball out of play to save. Bunyan, after the drop out, dribbled to Hawick grass and Reid ran within their 25, Morrison stopped a rush by good tackling and then Rodd earned a free kick with no advantage to his side. Sanderson got away on Hawick grass and when he was pulled down by Rodd, Bunyan picked up the ball and went over amidst much excitement. Turnbull took the kick and added to the Rose total. On resuming, Wilson had a run and chucked to Rodd who passed the 25 flag. Melrose were relieved but Hawick again reached the same place. From a throw forward they got near the uprights but Reid relieved with a long punt and then the whistle blew, leaving Melrose the victors of a game that had to be stopped several times on account of the excitement of the spectators. They were awarded the gold medals and Hawick the silver ones but whether the latter have accepted them as coming up to the standard of value we have not ascertained.

Prior to the 1891 tournament, the normal system of scoring had been only goals and tries counted, with one goal counting as more than any number of tries. The new system of scoring was as follows:

Try	2 points
Goal from try	3 points
Dropped goal	4 points
Penalty goal	2 points

At the same time, umpires who had previously been allowed on the pitch to help the referee were to stand on the touchline. This allowed the referee to take sole charge of the game, thus eliminating any decisions which could be disputed.

Before the 1892 Sports could take place, overnight snow was swept from the pitch, leaving the playing surface in very good condition. An object of interest was the new wooden pavilion the club had almost completed. The spacious balcony added both to its appearance and usefulness and was occupied during the day. A temporary grandstand had also been built, where Melrose Secretary W. Easton took up his viewing position. Although the rules stated that the second semi-finalists should receive ten minutes' rest-time, Hawick, very courteously, allowed Jedforest a 20-minute recovery period to get them into condition. Both sides had won convincingly on the way to the final and they started on level terms. The final was ten minutes each way and there was no scoring at half-time. In the second half T. Aimers charged forward and fed R. Scott, who raced in to score. A.B. Storrie failed with the easy kick.

By 1896, injuries were becoming a regular feature and, as at Mossilee the previous Saturday, the final turned out to be a tame, one-sided affair. Melrose were deprived of E.D. Hart, who was injured in the semi-final against Selkirk, and their six men were no match for Hawick. A second injury to J.L. Bogie reduced Melrose to five men and, realising the impossibility of their task, the remaining Melrose players left the field at 7.15 p.m. trailing 8–0 and the cup was handed to Hawick.

The 1890s were completely dominated by Hawick who appeared in every final except 1899. Their best year was 1894 when they recorded the Border Spring Sevens Grand Slam, winning at Gala, Melrose, Hawick and Jedforest. To give an indication of how strong Hawick were at that time, they provided all the backs for the South of Scotland team which that season beat Northumberland at Mansfield Park.

In 1899, Jedforest recorded their first success, narrowly defeating

Hawick – winners,
1894

Gala in the final. For long periods, Gala held the upper hand but Oliver and Barnes relieved the pressure for Jed and the latter was on hand to punt the ball upfield and win the race to the line. The winning team had a great reception on arrival at Jedburgh. There was a torchlight procession and Willie Oliver, the Jedforest captain, was carried through the town shoulder high.

Hawick returned to their winning ways in 1900 and were to appear in no fewer than 12 finals played between 1900 and 1914, but the outstanding team of the decade were Watsonians who won the cup in three successive years between 1905 and 1907.

The 1905 event was greatly enhanced by the inclusion of four Edinburgh teams and, more especially, the Watsonians who became the first City team to win at Melrose. No medals for the 1905 victors, they each received a handsome reading lamp, with the runners-up, Gala, each receiving a cruet stand.

The following match report in *The Kelso Chronicle* takes us back to how the Sports were viewed in 1905:

FOOTBALL SPORTS AT MELROSE

The second of the series, and undoubtedly the most important under the auspices of the Border Rugby Clubs, was held on Saturday, the rendezvous, as usual, being the Greenyards. This gathering has become very popular within the past few years, and a company numbering about 5,000 assembled around the ropes, while the two stands were also packed. The executives were again favoured with delightful weather – an ideal day for the game – and those present could not be disappointed with the Sport. The chief event, of course, was the seven-a-side tournament and this was greatly enhanced by the inclusion of four Edinburgh teams and, more especially, the Watsonians who were the first City team to carry away first prizes from the Border Sports, this being on the previous Saturday at Gala. The 'Sonians have now a thorough knowledge of the game, and they again proved successful on Saturday, having defeated Melrose, Jedburgh and Gala. The wearers of maroon and white displayed excellent form throughout and their victory was not only well-deserved, but a popular one. The programme also included three foot-racing events, for which there were good entries and these were well-contested, reflecting credit on the handicapper, Mr W.M. Badenoch. The arrangements were admirably carried through by Mr James E. Fairbairn, the energetic Secretary. The enjoyment of the proceedings was considerably enhanced by selections of St Boswells brass band and Melrose pipe and drum band.

Mr Edwin Boyd presided at the presentation of prizes, and said they were greatly indebted to the clerk of the weather for his kindness in allowing them to have their sports carried through under such favourable circumstances. As all well know, Melrose Sports had attained a high position in athletic circles, and more so that day, as Edinburgh teams had not only been well-represented, but had established a record by carrying away the cup for the first time. The Melrose team had often got through their preliminary tries but it was getting beyond a joke that they could not get into the final stage. However, all the teams had played well that day, and while no one could grudge the Watsonians their victory, it was much to be regretted that the final was fought out in semi-darkness, which was not justice to the spectators. Much had been said and written about the unpunctuality of teams taking the field, and he hoped that not only club matches would be started regularly in future, but that the final of their Sports would in another year be contested before darkness set in. The Melrose Club had always done their best to foster rugby football in the Borders and he hoped that the same friendly feeling would long exist between the City and Border clubs.

Although only eight clubs contested the 1905 tournament, surely a starting time of 4 p.m. was a bit on the late side. Watsonians recorded a hat trick of wins in 1907 when they defeated Clydesdale in the final. The Watsonians worked from the first tie like a well-oiled machine, and they were the favourites from the moment they disposed of Gala in the first round. They put in some splendid hand and foot work, with Cunningham giving a splendid lead in the scrum while Forbes, Angus and Spiers provided ample back-up.

Winning Watsonians team was as follows: H.J. Scougal, J.L. Forbes, J. Thorburn, A.W. Angus, L.M. Spiers, R.A. Gray and J.G. Cunningham.

The final of the 1908 tournament was contested between Hawick and Melrose who were appearing in their new, improved strip. Hawick won 3–0 but members of both the Hawick and Melrose teams received a gold medal.

Finalists

Hawick: J. Haig, T. Wilson, T. Neil, A. Burns, W.E. Kyle, T. Helm, J. Beattie.

Melrose: W. Logan, H.B. Tod, C. Gillie, W. Douglas, J.T. Fairbairn, A. Hope, A. Lockie.

The High Street of Melrose immediately after the presentation of the cup had never witnessed such an enthusiastic crowd. In the station, the evening crush was phenomenal and, when the Hawick team returned home, they were met by an immense coach, Peter Hope, the veteran trainer of the Greens, who was carried shoulder high from the station to the 'Horse'.

Hawick emulated Watsonians' feat of winning three successive tournaments in 1910, but it was not a happy afternoon for Melrose Treasurer J. Brown. On the morning of the Sports, the weather broke down and the crowd was down on the previous year. This was reflected in the takings which amounted to £150, a fall of £99 on the previous year. Royal High School led the City challenge with wins over Melrose and Gala, but Hawick were too strong and took the final 8–0.

Hawick: W.R. Sutherland, C. Ogilvy, T. Wilson, W. Burnet, G.W.T. Laing, W.E. Kyle, G. Johnstone.

The 1912 tournament was won by Hawick for the fifth successive year. The rugby football tournament kicked-off at 3 o'clock and the crowd exceeded 6,000. Extra seats had to be placed in front of the stand. Clydesdale failed to turn up so the host club quickly arranged for a B seven to take the field, but they were first into the bath, losing 18–0 to Heriots. The Edinburgh holiday weekend had brought down a large contingent from the capital. However, it was old Borders adversaries Hawick and Gala who battled it out for the coveted trophy.

The Kelso Chronicle, 19 April 1912, describes the final:

GALA V. HAWICK

With these popular teams in the final, the crowd round the ropes never thinned and each was received with a tremendous ovation. Nothing sensational happened until Sutherland looked a certain

Hawick – winners of the Spring Sevens Grand Slam, 1912

scorer but he overbalanced himself and was held. Tod worked the ball up touch and he and Thorburn had an interchange of passes. Kyle has seemingly taken up the fly-kicking game, and he repeatedly gained ground by kicking to touch. Each side possessed a flyer and it looked like an answer to the general desire when a race between Watson and Hunter took place. Watson, about ten yards behind, made after him and hauled him down about 15 yards from the goal-line amid deafening cheering. Hunter was probably handicapped with the ball, and he had also done a lot more work than Watson that afternoon but his fatal mistake was to turn round and see if his pursuer was gaining. The score was briefly delayed as Thorburn got across, and Tod kicked the goal. This first score raised the hopes of the Gala supporters but Hawick began to assert themselves and from about half-way Burnet took advantage of an opening and scored himself. He missed the kick, which still left Gala with the lead by two points. With a short kick and dribble, Lindsay Watson picked up the ball while running hard and put Hawick in front by scoring between the posts. Again Burnet missed the easy kick and at half-time the score was Hawick 6 Gala 5. The heavy Hawick forwards opened the second half with a rush to the Gala line, where Tod saved smartly but not to be denied, the Teries increased their lead through Shannon who scored by jumping an opponent and falling over the line. Another three points was the result of the kick as the angle was very awkward. From near midfield, Sutherland got away again with one of his characteristic runs which delight the Hawick supporters, dodging and swerving the opposing defence and ultimately scoring far out.

The seven-a-side football sports held at Melrose in 1915 were known as the Khaki tournament. All the teams engaged were drawn from military units, and a large proportion of the gathering around the ropes were clothed in khaki. Melrose Football Club, like all the other Border clubs, decided that they would not hold sports that season. A proposal to hold military sports instead seemed also doomed to failure when Colonel Sir R. Waldie Griffith and Lieut. Colonel McNeile stepped into the breach by guaranteeing to make good any deficit to make it possible for the Sports to go ahead. Unfortunately, although the railway company ran special trains from various other towns they could not grant special fares. Nevertheless, a crowd of 4,000 with a large military contingent gathered for the first match between 2/5th Royal Scots and the Forth Royal Garrison Artillery. Advantage was taken of the Sports to help some of the war-relief funds and also in further recruiting. The final was between the Lothian and Borders Horse A and the Royal Scots.

Lothian and Borders Horse A: A.J.M. Smith (Kelso), W.R. Sutherland (Hawick), J.A. Mann (Stewarts), A.P. Turnbull (Hawick), L.J. Clark (Gala), A. Macnab (Stewarts), W.D.L. Cullen (Academicals).

Royal Scots: J.P. Robbie (Wanderers), W.S. MacFarlane (Wanderers), L.C. Gordon (Heriots), A.B. Sinclair (Heriots), J.W.K. Darling (Merchiston), E. Littlejohn (Heriots), D.G. Ednie (Heriots).

THE INTER-WAR YEARS
I 1919–1930

The outstanding seven-a-side team of the 1920s were Hawick, and probably the finest exponent of the sevens game of his day and one of the great sevens scrum-halves was 'Andra' Bowie who won a record 54 senior seven-a-side medals. Bowie and R.N.R. Storrie made one of the most formidable sevens half-backs. Surprisingly, neither was capped at the 15-a-side game but if there had been international sevens in the 1920s, their names would have been first on the team sheet. Neither was particularly fast but when it came to a tournament on a Saturday, they were without equal. Bill McLaren takes up the tale:

> The stories of their craft are legion and like so many such tales they have, no doubt, been exaggerated over the years. Two examples illustrate the point. It even has been said – though it simply isn't true – that once, in the fading light of a particularly tense final, Bowie sold a dummy to the scrummage – in other words, didn't put the ball in at all – then darted off on the blind side for the vital try. What is absolutely true is that, in somewhat similar conditions, Bowie left the ball at the heels of his forwards while darting away on the blind side with his opposite number in hot pursuit, while Storrie picked up the ball and was through a barn-door gap to score with their opponents completely flummoxed.

After a lapse of four years, the time-honoured Sports returned to the Greenyards in 1919 and, despite the limited railway facilities, a large crowd lined the ropes. The gathering took the form of a purely seven-a-side contest, for which ten teams entered. Hawick and Jedforest met in the final and there was no scoring in the first period. In the second half R. Naylor scored an unconverted try for the Greens and shortly afterwards W.B. Aimers added a second, which Naylor goaled. The final result was Hawick 8 Jedforest 0.

The teams of the finalists are worth recording for the towns-people of Hawick and Jedburgh since so many people in these Border burghs have the same surnames.

Finalists

Hawick: R. Scott, W.B. Aimers, A. Bowie, R. Turnbull, T.R. Morgan (Captain), R. Thomson, R. Naylor.

Jedforest: J. Bruce, J. Scott, W. Scott (Captain), J. Telfer, W.B. Coltherd, J. Sinton, G. Hall.

Despite a bitterly cold spring afternoon, the 1920 tournament attracted a huge attendance and the athletics event, which had been so popular before the war, returned in the form of a one-mile handicap race which was run between the semi-final and the final. Border peds took the first three places but when you consider that the winning time was 4 minutes 49 seconds from a start of 110 yards, it gives an indication of how much sportsmen have improved over the last 70 years.

Result

1. J.W. Currie – Gala Harriers.
2. L.K. Millar – Gala Harriers.
3. T.W. Cuthbertson – Teviotdale Harriers.

Twelve teams took part in the seven-a-side contest, but the play was not up to the standard of the pre-war years. Stewarts College FP were the outstanding team of the day, although Hawick pressed them very hard in the final. A try by Stewarts winger I. Tait was all that separated the two sides.

Stewarts: I. Tait, T.R. Tod, C.V. Hendry, J.A. Mann, F. Kenedy, J.R.C. Buchanan, A.D. Lambert.

In 1921, the 35th Annual Sports took place, which was attended by an estimated 7,000 spectators. Excellent arrangments had been made by the Secretaries, Messrs W.J. Turner, G. MacKenzie and R. Mitchie, and the programme of events included – besides the seven-a-side rugby contest – place and drop-kick competitions, a dribbling race and foot racing. Twelve teams, including five from Edinburgh, took part and there were some unexpected results, such as the defeat of Gala by Melrose and the sensational win of Kelso over the much-fancied Jed side who had accounted for Hawick in the previous round. The final between Royal High School and Kelso was between the heaviest and the lightest teams and, although Kelso had the crowd behind them, they were overpowered by the Edinburgh side by a goal and four tries – 17 points to a goal (5 points).

Royal High School: E. McLaren, J.P. O'Donnell, R.J. Wheatley, J. Hume, D.S. Gay (F. Henry), K.F. Carmichael.

With the return of better railway facilities in 1922, the famous Melrose enclosure housed a crowd of 8,000, which broke all previous records, a credit to Melrose President Mr A. Brown. Melrose reached their first final since 1908. The early exchanges were confined to the Hawick half and J. Bunyan almost went over for Melrose. In a subsequent move, Melrose might have scored if Bunyan, at scrum-half, had sent the ball out. There was no scoring during normal time and extra time had to be played. J. Murray, the Hawick hooker, broke clear and added yet another to Hawick's many successes at the Greenyards.

The 1923 final between Heriots and Gala was one of the most exciting during the 1920s. Gala opened the scoring with a fine move involving G.R. Turner, J. Beattie and A. Walker before A. Murdison scored. Heriots equalised when K.S. Arthur, their winger, gathered the ball and touched down after a splendid run. Turner put Gala ahead for a second time but Murdison's attempted conversion fell short. Arthur notched his second try for Heriots and D. Drysdale put his team ahead by the narrow margin of 8–6. Heriots, the current Scottish champions, had won the Melrose Sevens for the first time and were popular winners.

The pre-eminent event in Border rugby reached a new plateau in 1924. The new stand was packed to capacity and a crowd of 10,000 paid a record £500 to witness 14 teams compete for Scotland's greatest rugby prize. With such a galaxy of rugby talent on view, including seven Scottish internationalists, the afternoon's play was a credit to the seven-a-side game and the crowd were treated to a feast of rugby. Three teams stood out from the rest: Hawick, Jedforest and Stewarts, with Hawick emerging as the victors. Lucky Hawick, claimed the neutrals. It took a titanic extra-time struggle to dispose of Stewarts in the semi-final, and only a goal-kick separated Hawick and Jedforest in the final. Gray and Bowie were outstanding for Hawick in their back divison with Amos proving to be one of the best forwards on view. In I.S. Smith, the Jed seven contained the outstanding personality of the Sports. Known as the flying Scotsman, he formed a formidable partnership with G.R.S. MacPherson of Edinburgh Accies in a dark-blue jersey.

The last-minute withdrawal of Edinburgh Wanderers necessitated the host club fielding a B seven in the 1925 tournament, but this did not prevent the famous old Abbey town being packed with thousands of rugby enthusiasts. Hawick, once again, proved they were the best by winning their third Melrose tournament in four years. The best tie of the afternoon was the thrilling second semi-final between Heriots and Gala with the Goldenacre side squeezing through by 14–13. That gruelling game with Gala had taken the sting out of the Heriots attack, while an injury to winger J.M. Wyllie made victory for Hawick all the easier. Bowie opened the scoring for Hawick and D.S. Davies converted. Further tries by Stevenson, Cairns and Gray took the score to 14–3 for Hawick. The forward trio of Davies, Cairns and Stevenson carried the Greens to victory, with Heriots the only team to cross the Hawick line. A.H. Brown, the Heriots scrum-half, was a warm favourite with the crowd and it would not be long before he would wear the coveted navy-blue jersey.

A crowd of 10,000 spectators gathered for the 1926 tournament and the brilliant weather had attracted large crowds from Edinburgh as well as the other Border towns. Gate receipts amounted to £750, which constituted a new record for the gathering.

A capital afternoon's sport was the general verdict as the crowd squeezed their way out of the Greenyards. For the neutral, it was good to see a name other than Hawick go on the trophy and, in R.F. Kelly and W. Whitelaw, Watsonians had the two best backs on view. For the Myreside Club it was their fifth success at Melrose, which was both popular and well merited. The Hawick supporters had to endure some anxious moments in the first round against

Stewarts College, and it took a late finish from those two Teri schemers Bowie and Storrie to get them out of jail. An injury to Storrie in the final against Watsonians contributed to their downfall and Watsonians took the cup by defeating Hawick 8–3. Other individuals to catch the eye were L.S. Kinnear of Stewarts College, A.T. Bain of Royal High School and Jock Allan of Melrose.

A sharp shower had made the ground a bit greasy for the 1927 final and darkened skies saw the last few minutes of the Hawick–Stewarts clash take place in almost total darkness. A.L. Fraser gave Stewarts the lead which C.W. Carmichael converted and T. Morrison was not far away with a drop-goal attempt. A. Bowie, who had first appeared at Melrose in 1919, proved that he was still a sevens maestro by running in for two tries with R.N.R. Storrie completing the Hawick scoring. The large Hawick following were now swarming on the touchline, waiting to celebrate their historic 17th victory.

In 1928, few people expected to see a final between Kelso and Edinburgh Accies, but at least it ensured that a new name would be inscribed on the Melrose Cup. In G.W. Dacker and G.P.S. Macpherson, Edinburgh Accies had two match-winners. Dacker was one of the fastest backs on display and his direct running brought several tries. By contrast Macpherson, the Oxford Blue and Scotland international, threaded his way through the opposition with his swerving runs. However, it was hooker J.A. Wright who secured the vital score in the final against Kelso.

The 1929 seven-a-side tournament was played in glorious conditions and a crowd of 10,000 were treated to an all-Border final between Hawick and Gala. The Borders were represented by seven teams and Edinburgh provided the remaining seven. Among those present were six of the winning Melrose seven of 40 years earlier: G. Brown, D. Sanderson, G. Bunyan, R. Murdieson, W. Reid and J. Turnbull.

The huge crowd were treated to a fine afternoon's sport and, after a couple of Edinburgh victories in the two opening ties at the expense of Kelso and Jedforest, the Border clubs came into their own. Hawick had a splendid victory over Edinburgh Academicals, the cup holders and the winners of the Murrayfield tournament the previous Saturday. The Hawick forward trio of W.B. Welsh, J. Beattie and R. Knox denied Accies the possession they needed and the dual danger of Dacker and Macpherson was snuffed out. Both Gala and Hawick Sevens received rapturous applause when they took the field for the final. Beattie opened the scoring for Hawick but Storrie missed the conversion attempt. Gala equalised when J.T. Gill raced over the Hawick line. Unfortunately for the Braw Lads, T.G. Aitchison's kick was charged down. Gala took the lead when J.H. Ferguson dashed over for a try, but once again a Hawick forward touched the ball in its flight over the bar and no goal was again the result. R.A.V. Grieve went over in the corner to tie the score at six-all in the closing minute and, amid great Teri jubilation, Welsh landed a magnificent goal from the touchline to give Hawick victory 8–6.

The traditional high standard of play associated with the Melrose gathering was fully maintained in 1930 when Edinburgh Academicals lifted the trophy for the second time in three years. From their very first score in their initial appearance against Selkirk, they were established as firm favourites, and although each member of the team played their part, it was largely due to the generalship and superior skills of G.P.S. Macpherson. The Scottish captain was in inspired form and, once again, Dacker was not slow to profit from his captain's good work.

B.R. Tod and G.M. Crabbie were the best half-back combination on view, and the Accies forwards ensured a sufficient supply of ball to ensure that their backs could win their ties with something to spare. Heriots were worthy runners-up – in A.H. Brown, they had one of the outstanding individual performers, and M. Robson, the England international, was prominent in defence.

THE INTER-WAR YEARS
II 1931–1945

Although Melrose had won their own sevens three times during the nineteenth century, it was not until 1931 that they won the cup which was first played for in 1895. It was their first Border Sevens success since 1910. The place-kicking and drop-kicking competitions were popular sideshows with the crowd and this year they were evenly contested between the Allan brothers of Melrose.

Place-Kick	1.	H. Allan, Melrose
	2.	J.W. Allan, Melrose
Drop-Kick	1.	C. Mitchell, Melrose
	2.	J.W. Allan, Melrose
Dribbling Race	1.	R. Wilson, Melrose
	2.	D. Bunyan, Melrose

The Wasps were very much the underdogs when they faced Hawick in the final. The previous Saturday Hawick had won the Gala Sevens and Andrew Bowie collected his 50th Sevens medal. Jock Allan gave the home side an inspiring lead, but the hero for Melrose was winger W.J. Nisbet who scored two tries to give Melrose an 11–6 win. Jock Allan, who had recently converted five tries for Scotland in the Calcutta Cup match at Murrayfield, was top scorer with one try and seven goals.

The 1932 tournament was known as the Jubilee Sports and Walter Thomson, better known as 'Fly Half' in *The Sunday Post*, fondly recalls the day:

I had the privilege of reporting the Jubilee Sevens but not from the sybaritic comfort of the present press box, which was in a sense spawned at the Jubilee Sevens, but from a table and chair set out on the touchline near the turnstiles with the rain unceasing for five sodden hours and a notebook resembling a trainer's sponge. The weather perhaps was a judgment on Melrose for daring to celebrate their jubilee a year too soon. It is difficult now to recall the intensity with which rugby was followed in the Borders. There were no distractions. One spoke of nothing but the sevens for weeks before – and of little else for weeks after. For hadn't Melrose, always the most enterprising of entrepreneurs, chosen to lift their tournament to a higher rung by inviting the mighty Barbarians to be their first major guest side? It was a great coup and the names of these wondermen were awaited with anticipation – and trepidation.

Drawn from the cream of England, Ireland and Wales, with six caps in their midst, it seemed that the day would be dedicated to the pursuit of runners-up. Everyone knew where the cup would go. But it didn't work out like this at all. The weather took a hand, leaving the pitch like a bog and pouring heaven's hard on the 8,000 spectators without a hint of remission. My abiding memory of the conditions was provided at the finish of the Gala–Hawick semi-final. Victory went to Gala by 3–0 and, perhaps secretly relieved that release was at hand, that rotund citizen of Hawick, Jerry Foster, keeled over and sank, as someone unkindly said, in the swamp, like a ruddy hippopotamus. The record skid of the day was credited to F.M. Matheson, the Gala wing, who slid 15 yards, taking his tackler with him.

In such conditions the form book could be thrown away. The greatest upset came in the other semi-final where Kelso were whipped into such a frenzy by that Hambiyant farmer from Kaimflat, Jimmy Graham, that they beat the Barbarians. No wonder the Eildons trembled. The effort left Kelso drained and they were beaten by Gala in the final by two typical opportunist tries by that laconic half-back W.W. Barbour. When it was all over, and we had begun to dry out, the prime talking-point was that astonishing performance by Kelso. How odd that when the Barbarians next appeared at the Greenyards they should lose again, short of the final, to Kelso with Jimmy Graham's son in the side. But, then, Melrose Sports are full of odd bits of family history. When Gala won that Jubilee tournament Henry Polson, the first Braw Lad, stood shoulder to shoulder with the undoubtable Jimmy Ferguson. Polson's dad had been in the Gala Seven when they last won at Melrose in 1903.

Above: Melrose – winners, 1931

Below: Veterans of the 1883 winning Melrose side at the 1932 Jubilee Sports

*Hawick – winners at
a Gala, Melrose and
Hawick, 1933*

By 1933, the popularity of the Sports had extended beyond the Borders. Special trains were laid on from Edinburgh and a record crowd of 12,000 saw the cup going to Hawick. The new press box at the Greenyards was an impressive sight and a source of great interest to the crowd.

After sharing the Scottish Championship with Dunfermline and retaining the Border Cup, Hawick proved to be the best balanced seven at the Greenyards and their splendid teamwork, plus a great display of grit and will to win fully justified their success. W.B. Welsh was their outstanding forward and he was ably supported by J. Beattie and R.W. Barrie. Among the backs A.E. Fiddes put in a splendid afternoon's work and ended the day with four tries and seven conversions. G.W. Reid provided Fiddes with solid service and the elusive running of R.N.R. Storrie, especially in the final against Gala, also contributed to Hawick's victory.

In 1934, Royal High School won the cup for the second time in their history by defeating Kelso 20–0 in the final. The outstanding tie of the afternoon took place in the semi-final when Royal High School and Hillhead High School, the joint champions of Scotland, took to the field in the first semi-final. J.L. Cotter, the Hillhead and Scotland stand-off, had a pass intercepted by R.C. Logan and this snap try by the Royal High School centre was sufficient to carry the school through. With two internationals in their backs, in J. Park and W.D. Emslie, Royal High were too strong for Kelso in the final.

Glorious weather favoured the premier Border seven-a-side Sports in 1935 and, as usual, there were 16 teams taking part. Glasgow were not represented on this occasion but a seven representing London Scottish were attractive newcomers.

The early ties had been drab affairs, but by the semi-final stage there were no Border sides left. The semi-final tie between London Scottish and Heriots was one of the best seen during the 1930s. The Anglos were leading by six points but a jinking run by J.F. Lawrie and some cleverly conceived moves initiated by E.J. Oxley, a real sevens personality at the time, rattled in 11 points to leave the Scottish with a minute left to strive for the equaliser. R.W. Dunn and M.L. Lucas spread-eagled the Heriots defence and Lucas scored the winning try in extra time.

The other semi-final, between Watsonians and Edinburgh Accies, was another close affair, with the Scottish champions

Watsonians emerging as victors. E.G.L. Mark, the Watsonians stand-off, was the architect behind their success and not far behind him was the burly and resolute E.C. Hunter at three-quarter. G.W. Anderson provided Mark with an immaculate service at scrum-half. Of the forwards, veteran W.C. Morrison saw to it that the back division were well supplied with the ball. In a one-sided final, Watsonians overran a tired-looking exiles side by 16–3. It would be another 27 years before a London Scottish side would win Melrose.

Watsonians returned the following year to successfully defend the trophy they had won and a crowd of over 12,000 packed into the famous Melrose enclosure. Edinburgh was taking over as the rugby capital of Scotland, and the fact that Melrose were the only Border club to survive the first round was an indication that the superiority of the Borderers was coming to an end.

J.M. Johnstone, W.C. Morrison and G.B. Hendry gave an exemplary display as a forward unit. R.H. Dryden, on the wing, was given ample opportunity to show his pace and the Edinburgh flyer obliged with seven touchdowns. At stand-off E.G.L. Mark was always one step ahead of his opponents, and at the base of the scrum G.W. Anderson supplemented his clever play by a very marked efficiency in goal-kicking. However, the player of the tournament was undoubtedly Watsonians three-quarter, E.C. Hunter.

The presence of the brothers J.R. and A.T. Stewart in the Melrose Seven, the former a Cambridge Blue, was a great factor in the progress of the Greenyards side to the final. G.M. Dobson did well at scrum-half for the Rose while R. Cowe, up until the final, looked the outstanding forward on view. However, Watsonians became the first side to run up 30 points in a Melrose final and comfortably defeated the host side by 33–0.

Memory Match A.B. Tod, Gala, 1937

Taking his seat at the Greenyards at this year's sevens was A.B. Tod, one of the few surviving members of the victorious Gala Seven of 1937. Still a regular attender at Netherdale for Gala's home matches, the popular Gala baker has fed four generations of Gala rugby players with his famous pies:

'I have always had a soft spot for Melrose. My father, H.B. Tod, captained both Melrose and Gala before the First World War and was picked for Scotland in 1911. It was a very kind gesture by the Melrose Committee in 1987 when they invited Tom Carruthers and myself to make the 1987 draw, 50 years after we had won the Sports.

'The game of rugby has changed a great deal since my day and I admire the dedication of the players of today who have got to put so much time into the game. There were no bars, fitness-rooms, floodlights and the like in those days. Training would consist of six to eight laps round the Public Park under the old gas streetlights. For an away match in Edinburgh, we would take the train to Waverley and meet in the old St Andrew Square Hotel and get a bus to wherever we were playing. We would then come back to the hotel and be served fish and chips, and bacon and eggs. Today you see players warming up an hour before the kick-off. If we were playing at home with a three o'clock starting time, ten to three would be early enough to arrive.

'We had done well to reach the final and most people expected us to lose to London Scottish. They had the vastly experienced Scottish stand-off in H. Lind and two caps in the forwards G.B. Horsburgh and D.A. Titon.

'There were two major differences to the way in which the game is played today. You were offside if you were in front of the ball, and forwards did not handle the ball – they dribbled it. I don't remember much about the final except that we were losing 11–8 and there was not long to go. Tom Carruthers dribbled the ball from midfield and scored in front of the posts. The conversion went over and the referee blew his whistle. It was a long time before Gala were to win at Melrose again. Sadly, our team did not last – J. Dun was killed in active duty and J.S. Lawrie died in a Far East prisoner of war camp.'

In one of the most thrilling inter-war year finals, Heriots won the 1938 Sports by defeating Edinburgh Academicals by 10–5. In their four ties, Heriots FP scored 46 points against 14 and, although J.B. Craig scored four tries, every other member of the Heriots side contributed to their tally. A fascinating contest on the wing took place between Craig and R.E. Harvey, with the Accies man winning the early exchanges. However, Oxley was soon in the thick of things, dribbling over for a try which was converted by J.H.G. Napier. C. Ritchie scored a brilliant try for the Accies by beating the Heriots defence and B.R. Todd levelled the scores. Napier sent Craig flying in at the posts to give Heriots a half-time lead. The second half started at great pace but, with defences on top for both sides, there was no further scoring and the cup was destined for Goldenacre.

According to local form and general expectations, the Heriots Seven repeated their success of 1938 and the coveted trophy returned to Edinburgh for the fifth time in the 1930s. It was also a repeat of last year's final, with Edinburgh Accies the bridesmaids for the second time. Defeating Watsonians, London Scottish and Hawick *en route* to the final, Heriots fielded the same seven who had won the previous years. This was the best seven to appear at Melrose before the war. In Oxley, Brown and Deas, they had forwards who could run and win ball all day. Napier knew all the tricks of the trade at three-quarter and he made full use of his young and speedy colleague Craig on the wing. Brydon at scrum-half was the player of the tournament with a number of blind-side breaks, while T. Gray opened up defences for his faster colleagues outside him. It was unfortunate that the second best team at Melrose that day were knocked out in the first tie by Heriots. Had Watsonians stand-off A. Reid been successful with a second-half penalty attempt, the Myreside men would have taken Heriots to extra time.

Memory Match D.W. Deas, Heriots and Scotland, 1940

Along with Sam Oxley, Wallace Deas was one of the great personalities who played at Melrose during the 1930s. Like so many players of his generation, his representative rugby was curtailed by the war and it was not until 1947 that Wallace won his first cap, against France. He won the first of his three Melrose Medals in 1938 and he and Glen Napier played in all three victories.

'I always enjoyed playing at Melrose. In those days, it was the first Border Sevens of the Circuit for the Edinburgh sides, because we played at Murrayfield the Saturday before rather than Gala. The Greenyards pitch always looked lush compared to the City grounds at the end of the season, especially around the touchlines. When you got on to the pitch you realised that the bare bits had been covered by newly cut gass.

'The 1940 tournament was my third Melrose victory but we did not receive any medals that year. However, we were presented with our winners' medals nearly 50 years later, and it was a very emotional moment when we went down to Melrose to collect them. There were not many of us left.

'I was a teenager when I first played at Melrose but our headmaster at the time did not like the schoolboys playing sevens with the FPs. In fact, the first time I ever played sevens was at Melrose.

'In those days, Heriots was a closed club so the chaps we played rugby with were all former school chums. Most of us were keen footballers and our training nights were mainly spent playing five-a-side football. This gave us two advantages. It kept us fit and we were probably the first side to have a set of forwards who were quite comfortable handling the ball.

'Most of us have a favourite Melrose story and mine concerns the former SRU President Alex Brown. There was a big military display at Edinburgh Castle with the Army, Navy, RAF and police, all represented by their bigwigs. A senior military man displaying all his medals was approached by Alex who said, "Ah see ye havnae got a Melrose Medal there."

'The 1940 tournament was depleted slightly with so many players in the forces and 14 teams took part. As usual, the seven Border clubs were represented and six Edinburgh clubs took part, with the Accies and the Wanderers merging to reach the semi-final. Dunfermline were the other guest side. We defeated Selkirk, Melville College and Accies/Wanderers to reach the final. Ian Cochrane had replaced Tommy Gray at stand-off and the 1940 tournament will be remembered as Ian's final. He scored three tries in the final against Watsonians as well as dropping a goal. We went on to win 18–3.

'The 1950 tournament also has happy memories for me. It was the last time I played at Melrose and we lost 9–0 to Melrose in the semi-final. I was delighted that Charlie Drummond won his first Melrose Medal. We had made our Scotland débuts together. It was also the one and only time I played at Melrose with my younger brother.

'Despite the worsening wartime situation, Melrose again managed to host a wartime competition in 1941, which was won by Edinburgh City Police, defeating Gala by 13–3 in the final. Most teams were weakened due to active service but don't mention that to former Chief Constable of Lothian and Borders Police Sir John Orr. As PC J.H. Orr, the former SRU President was a member of the victorious police line-up:

Joining the Police Force a few months after witnessing the great Gala victory of 1937, my dreams of ever playing at Melrose seemed destined never to be fulfilled but, in 1941, that prized invitation arrived. Despite service commitments, the Melrose Committee organised a full programme and it spoke volumes for the attraction of Melrose that so many prominent players managed to organise leave in order to participate. On a hectic afternoon we played Jedforest, Royal High, Hawick and beat a Gala side containing such well-known characters as Alistair Caskie, Duggie Mitchell and George Lyall in the final. In accordance with wartime practice, no medals were awarded – but who cared.

For the last of the wartime tournaments a 16-team competition was resumed but there were some unfamiliar names in the starting line-up. The RAF East Fortune team could not raise seven players and were replaced by Melrose Co-optimists. Other first-round casualties included RAF Charterhall, Musselburgh, Lasswade, Royal Dick Vet College, Royal Navy and a Combined Services Seven which contained six caps. Hawick were represented by two teams, the Combined Trades and the Hawick Borderers. It was the latter who claimed the scalp of Surgeon Lieut. D.W.D. MacLennan's Combined Services team. However, the Hawick Borderers were to fall at the final hurdle to a young Watsonians side.

THE POST-WAR YEARS
1946–1959

The 1946 tournament was the first held at the Greenyards after the end of the Second World War and Hawick recorded their 24th win, defeating the host side Melrose in the final 3–0. The sevens that year were held over for a week and took place on Saturday 20 April because the previous Saturday Scotland had defeated England 27–0 in a victory international.

In their four ties Hawick only scored five tries with none of these being converted. The final was also a dour, low-scoring affair. Melrose had the better of the exchanges in the first half and A. Crawford was unlucky to see a penalty attempt drift just wide of the upright. However, Hawick winger W.R. Scott scored against the run of play and Hawick were able to hold on until the final whistle. On their way to the final, Hawick defeated city rivals Heriots FP, Watsonians and Stewarts FP, with E. Anderson of Stewarts FP the only person to cross the Hawick line that afternoon. W.R. Scott scored four of the Hawick tries with scrum-half, J.R. McCredie going over for the other.

The following year, for the first time since 1931, Melrose won their own Sports in one of the most thrilling post-war finals, defeating Stewarts FP 11–8 after eight minutes of extra time. Two dropped goals from Melrose stand-off D.M. Hogg disposed of Watsonians in the first round before narrow wins over local rivals Selkirk and Kelso took Melrose into their second successive final. In the final, Stewarts FP took the lead when winger A.E. Bennet scored for J.W.C. Foubister to convert. T. Hook replied with a score between the posts for Melrose but the vital conversion was missed. However, with his bewildering sidestep A.R. Frater scored again for Melrose and D.M. Hogg was successful with the conversion. With

Melrose holding on to an 8–5 lead, Foubister broke through the Melrose defence to level the scores. The hushed crowd waited for Foubister to goal his own try, but from way out the kick was unsuccessful and extra time loomed. In a pulsating extra period, Melrose centre A.R. Frater, dubbed the best uncapped centre of the 1950s, sent the crowd into ecstasy when he finally pierced the Stewarts FP defence.

In 1948 Melrose won their own sevens for a second successive year, defeating Kelso 11–8 in the final. This was sweet revenge for the home side who had lost to Kelso by 13–5 in the final of the Gala Sevens the previous Saturday. The day did not begin well for the home side when Melrose legend C.W. Drummond had to call off due to injury but W. Rankin, appearing in his first Melrose final, was to prove an inspired replacement, helping himself to no fewer than five tries during the afternoon, including two in the final against Kelso which swept Melrose into an early eight-point lead. Kelso replied with a try from forward D.M. Welsh and G. Wilson before J. Simpson wriggled his way in at the corner for the winning Melrose score.

The 1949 tournament was not a happy afternoon for Border clubs with five out of seven falling at the first hurdle. Hawick managed to reach the first semi-final, only to fall 5–0 to Stewarts FP, with Edinburgh Accies defeating guest side London Scottish in the other semi-final. The loudest cheer of the afternoon had been reserved for the Scottish football team who had just beaten England 3–1 at Wembley.

With an all-Edinburgh final, the attendance had thinned but spectators who stayed were treated to one of the best open finals. W.I.D. Elliot opened the scoring for Edinburgh Accies behind the posts, giving D.A. Sloan an easy conversion. That wily old sevens campaigner E. Anderson scored for Stewarts and A.S. McDonald levelled with the goal. With extra time looming, W.I.D. Elliot outpaced the Stewarts defence, scoring in spectacular fashion to give the Accies their first triumph since 1930.

Uncertain weather, a cold, blustering day and persistent showers restricted the attendance at the 1950 tournament but this did not prevent Melrose from winning their own cup for the third time in four years. In the early rounds Heriots had caught the eye with an impressive 20–3 win over a London Scottish team which included a certain F.H. Coutts. In A.M. Mason, Heriots had a real flyer. However, telepathic play by the Hogg brothers and the marking of A.M. Mason by C.W. Drummond eased Melrose into the final to play Watsonians who had defeated Hawick in the other semi-final. In the final, J. Hogg chipped ahead to put Melrose ahead before C.W. Drummond scored the winning try. In a family affair, D.M. Hogg received the coveted trophy from his wife.

The 1950s represented a new era for the Scottish sportsman. The media ensured that they became household names. Hibs may have had the famous five – Smith, Johnstone, Reilly, Turnbull and Ormond; Hearts may have had the trio of Conn, Bauld and Wardhaugh; but, equally, everyone had heard of the Melrose back division – Frater, Drummond and the Hogg brothers.

Making their first appearance in the Melrose seven-a-side tournament in 1951 were Rosslyn Park, who became the first club to take the Melrose Cup south of the border. (Tyndale, the only other English club to have won at Melrose, had achieved this feat in 1886 when no trophy was awarded.) Also making his début at Melrose that year was D.M. Brown, the only Melrose player with a complete set of Border medals, who joined old hands J. Johnston and W. Anderson in the Melrose front row. It was Melrose who were to give the Middlesex Sevens holders their hardest tie and it took a last-minute penalty goal from the touchline by Rosslyn Park hooker N.E. Williams to deny the host side a place in the semi-final. With Melrose the last Border side left in the competition, half of the estimated crowd of 10,000 had disappeared by 6 p.m. when Rosslyn Park and Heriots took the field for the final. In a rather dull match, it was the boot of Williams which put the English side ahead, and J.V. Smith, the flying Rosslyn Park winger, extended this lead to give his side an 8–0 cushion at the interval. W.G. Macmillan, the Heriots centre, reduced the leeway with a try converted by K.R. McMath but it proved to be a consolation score.

Memory Match J.L. Allan, Melrose, 1952

The 1951–52 season was a memorable one for both Melrose FC and Les Allan. Melrose were Scottish champions for the first time, Les won his first of four caps, against France, and he scored against the touring Springboks for the South of Scotland at Hawick. To make the season complete, he picked up his first Melrose Medal.

'Melrose had a great duel with Stewarts College FP that season, both in the 15s and in the sevens, and we duly found ourselves in the final with them at the Gala tournament. We were leading 13–3 at half-time and the uncommitted spectators were beginning to drift away, confident of a Melrose victory. Stewarts, however, had other ideas and I got a nice rear view of Grant Weatherstone as he scored a try just on the stroke of time. Clark Sharp converted to level the scores so it was into extra time. With the minutes ticking away and neither side looking like scoring, Stewarts were awarded a slightly mysterious penalty about the half-way line. As Clark Sharp thumped over the long-range kick, I think I suffered one of the worst moments of frustration I have ever experienced on a rugby field. However, there we were lining up for the presentations and I had a gut feeling that we were going to see more of Stewarts College the following week at Melrose. They had a fine seven with forwards Bill Ralph, Clark Sharp and Mike Robertson, Grant Weatherstone to run in the tries on the wing and backs Craigie Ross and Jack Foubister to make the openings and that maestro Ernie Anderson at scrum-half to orchestrate the whole thing. One of the very best in an age when good sevens scrum-halfs were a bit thicker on the ground than they are now.

'Melrose Sevens day 1952 turned out to be ideal weatherwise, and a near-capacity crowd turned up to see the next act in the Melrose v. Stewarts FP drama. The draw favoured us with the better half and my main memory of the first tie against Edinburgh Accies, apart from scoring a couple of tries, was of Alastair Frater being sick on the field and us doing our best to avoid that spot on the ground thereafter. It certainly didn't do him any lasting harm as he proved in running in three classic tries against Royal High whom we beat 15–5 in the semi-final. We scrambled a bit against Langholm in the second round, with Jimmy Maxwell and Hector Monro in their ranks. An extra-time win this was and I think I managed to bag at least one of the important tries.

'Meanwhile, Stewarts hadn't had their troubles to seek, needing to call on all their considerable sevens experience to defeat by 8–3, the holders Rosslyn Park, who contained in their ranks a future President of the RFU Mr J.V. Smith, who could run a bit in his day, and England centre Brian Boobyer, who had the most gorgeous shimmy of the hips as he took on his opposite number. In an agonising semi-final Stewarts got all the luck that was going against Heriots, beating them by 5–3. Winger W.G. Macmillan lost the ball over the line in the act of scoring and Heriots also missed an easy penalty.

'However, there we were lining up for the kick-off in the final, the main thought in our minds being that there must be no slip-ups like the previous week. Ivor Hogg, as ever the supreme opportunist, opened the scoring with a drop-goal. And then shortly afterwards, in a broken-play situation which epitomised the easy-going adaptability of the whole seven at that time, I slotted into stand-off to take a pass from hooker Bill Anderson who was deputising at the time for scrum-half Jim Hogg. Jim, meanwhile, found himself on the wing and when the ball eventually reached him he came inside the cover with an outrageous dummy/sidestep and scored between the posts. Ivor converted and we were 8–0 up at half-time and feeling good.

'Stewarts were anything but finished, and midway through the second half that man Weatherstone again got the ghost of an overlap, and as his long legs took him clear and behind the posts for Clark Sharp to convert – little niggling doubts and memories of the previous week kept cropping up. Back we came, however, and a kick and chase by Derek Brown and Jimmy Johnston saw the ball just elude Jimmy's desperate dive as it went over the dead-ball line at the Policeman's Corner. While we were still trying to gather our composure the Stewarts stand-off Jack Foubister, who was, as

Melrose – winners,
1952

ever, alive to the attacking potential of the situation, grabbed the ball, took a quick drop out and in a trice it was in the hands of Craigie Ross with Grant Weatherstone running free outside him. Desperately, I tried to stop Ross from getting the ball away but without success. As my spirits sank and Weatherstone got into his stride for what would undoubtedly have been the winning try, there came the sound of heavenly music – the whistle of the referee to signify a forward pass. To this day the Stewarts boys feel slightly aggrieved about the decision. As ever, there is only one opinion that counts, however, and referee Jack Taylor was certainly no sluggard when it came to getting about the field. As the minutes ticked away to the final whistle it was pretty desperate stuff and my last recollection of the final was of making a mark under our own posts with literally seconds to go, and then thumping the ball into St Mary's School hoping like hell that the ball boys would take their time. The final whistle went shortly afterwards to put us out of our agony and for yours truly it was a dream come true. For some of the others in the team it was their second or even third Melrose Medal. For me it was the first and it was precious.'

The 1953 tournament was held on one of the wettest Melrose Sevens days since the famous Jubilee event of 1932, and the attendance of 8,000 was the smallest since the war. However, Hawick gave one of their finest sevens displays to lift their first Melrose Cup since 1946. With a forward trio of J.J. Hegarty, H. McLeod and A. Robson, the key to the Hawick success was possession. Heriots, who were to emerge as a great seven in the late 1950s, gave Hawick their sternest test in a second-round tussle which went to the wire. Finalists Melrose, who were deprived of the services of J.L. Allan after a hard-fought first-round victory over Gala, were no match for Hawick who won the tries from W.R. Scott and N.G. Davidson with J. Wright adding a penalty and a conversion.

Wasps, the 1952 Middlesex winners, failed to impress. They scraped through their opening tie 5–0 against Edinburgh Accies but were despatched by Stewarts FP in the next round.

Heriots, for the first time since 1940, won the 1954 event fresh from their triumph at the Murrayfield Sevens the previous Saturday. A crowd of 9,000 were treated to an afternoon of exciting ties and shocks with Jedforest providing the biggest upset by knocking out the much-fancied London Scottish Seven in the first round. Close victories over Melrose and Edinburgh Wanderers took the Riverside club to their first post-war Melrose final. D.S. Dakers opened the scoring for Heriots with a typical scrum-half's try. P.S. Shearer converted. J.M.K. Weir extended their lead with an unconverted try, but the biggest cheer of the afternoon came when the Jed centre burst over to score. W.G. Macmillan strolled in for another try for Heriots who emerged comfortable winners.

By the mid-1950s four clubs began to dominate the Border Sevens Circuit, and it was no surprise that the semi-finalists of 1955 were Heriots, Hawick, Stewarts and Melrose. Ties between these clubs brought out great rivalry on the pitch and mutual respect and camaraderie off it. Not surprisingly, both semi-finals went to extra time with the tie between Heriots and Hawick proving to be a real nail-biter. Heriots took the lead through W.G. Macmillan after the versatile D.B. Edwards had dribbled through. P.S. Shearer added the goal. J.J. Hegarty reduced the deficit just after half-time but D.E. Muir scored to keep Heriots ahead. With time running out, a break by R.G. Charters gave J.H. Bowie the opportunity to tie things up at eight-all. Into extra time, Hawick were awarded a penalty and Bowie coolly stroked over the resulting kick. In a one-sided final, Hawick trounced Melrose by 28–3 with E. Broatch emerging as the top try scorer of the tournament with six touchdowns.

After appearing in countless semi-finals and finals of Border Sevens during the 1950s, Stewarts FP eventually secured the prize they were looking for when they captured the trophy in 1956. They had convincing wins over Melrose, Gala and Watsonians before beating Hawick 11–9 in a pulsating final. They scored 63 points in four ties, the Sharp brothers contributing no fewer than 42 points between them. The Combined Universities of Glasgow and Edinburgh played some fine, open rugby and were most unlucky to lose 8–6 to Hawick in the semi-final. The large crowd of 12,000 were anticipating a keenly contested final and they were not disappointed.

R.G. Charters opened the scoring for Hawick, only for J.C.M. Sharp to cancel this with a penalty goal. I. Fraser restored Hawick's lead when he nipped in for a try just before the interval. G.D. Stevenson, alias 'Stevie', was surrounded by three Stewarts opponents as he went up for a high ball but dived over in his own inimitable way, only for the ball to fall from his grasp. Fortunately, J.J. Hegarty was on hand to follow up and plunge over. J.C.M. Sharp brought Stewarts back into the game with a try to reduce the deficit to 9–6. With the seconds ticking away, G. Sharp equalised for Stewarts, scoring under the posts and leaving his brother the simple task of knocking over the winning goal.

The 1957 tournament will be remembered as the final spoiled by injuries. Stewarts FP had beaten Heriots FP in the final of the 1957 Murrayfield Sevens and these old Edinburgh adversaries were to contest the Melrose final a week later. The Combined Universities had once again entertained the crowd with their brand of open rugby, and hooking for the students that day was Edinburgh undergraduate N.G.R. Mair, who also had a spell with Melrose, but he was unable to prevent Heriots from reaching another Melrose final. Stewarts FP led by 10–5 at the break after Heriots had lost the services of D.B. Edwards for most of the first half. Just as Edwards resumed after treatment, the Stewarts scrum-half, G.M. Robertson, had to leave the field, and thereafter Heriots were able to puncture a six-man Stewarts defence at will and ran up 21 points in the second half to emerge as 26–10 victors. We shall never know what the outcome of this final would have been if both teams had been at full strength.

Just as Melrose had done a decade earlier, Heriots returned to the Greenyards in 1958 and successfully defended their title by defeating Langholm by 14–0 in the final. However, the tie of the day was the semi-final clash between Heriots and a Co-optimists side which boasted seven internationalists and two British Lions in A.R. Smith and A.J.F. O'Reilly. The Heriots forwards, D.W. Syme, R.M. Tollervey and D.B. Edwards, simply denied the Co-optimists possession. K.J.F. Scotland emerged as the top points scorer with 23 points, which consisted of two tries, seven conversions and a penalty goal. R.M. Tollervey was the only Heriots player not to get on the score sheet that afternoon but by denying the ball to Smith and O'Reilly he had more than done his share.

The last competition of the 1950s took place in sunshine on a dry pitch which was ideal for fast, flowing rugby. There were no guest teams that year and the tournament was made up by the seven Border clubs, eight teams from Edinburgh and Glasgow HSFP. Making his Melrose Sevens début that day was J.W. Telfer Esq. 1959 was to be the Year of the Braw Lad when Gala won for the first time since their historic win in 1937. Faced with the stiffer half of the draw, Gala defeated Kelso, Stewarts FP and Edinburgh Accies to reach the final. Melrose, who were without J.L. Allan and A.J. Hastie, both injured at Netherdale the previous Saturday, did well to reach the final but were never really in the hunt as Gala emerged as 9–3 victors. K.W. Anderson, the Gala stand-off, helped himself to 30 of the 51 points Gala had amassed that afternoon.

THE 1960s

If the 1950s had produced four clubs which were to dominate the Border Sevens Circuit during that era, the 1960s witnessed possibly four of the best teams ever to appear at the Greenyards.

Who could forget the K.J.F. Scotland inspired Cambridge University side of 1960? The London Scottish side of the early 1960s transformed the way in which rugby sevens was played, attracting capacity audiences wherever they appeared. In 1967 Hawick achieved a remarkable ten Border Sevens on the trot, beginning at Netherdale 1966, winning all the Spring and Autumn Sevens and repeating their Gala and Melrose victories the following year. But the decade was to end with the cup travelling south again to an English college. Loughborough Colleges were popular visitors and winners at Melrose, claiming the titles in 1968 and 1969.

Memory Match K.J.F. Scotland, Cambridge University, 1960

Ken Scotland was one of the outstanding rugby footballers of his generation. In a distinguished international career, in which he won 27 Scottish caps with no fewer than six clubs, and five Tests for the British Lions, he became the first player to win a Melrose medal with two clubs. His three Melrose medals are still among his most prized possessions:

'I returned to my parents' home in Edinburgh after the Lent Term had broken up at Cambridge and I received a telephone call from Charlie Drummond. "Ken, we would like you to send a team from Cambridge University to play at Melrose this year," he said. Fortunately, four of my team-mates were fellow Scots and were relatively easy to track down. Gordon Waddell and John Brash had learnt their rugby at Fettes, and Cameron Boyle had been to Merchiston, so there was a real Edinburgh connection to the side. I remember hiring an old Morris 1000 to bring down the Edinburgh contingent and we met up with Ronnie Thomson, Alan Godson and Mike Weston at Melrose as they had travelled up by train from the south.

'The *Edinburgh Evening News* at the time gave us no chance and were wondering why the Melrose Committee were paying our expenses when we were drawn against Hawick in the first round. How could we possibly get any possession when the Hawick forwards were Jack Hegarty, Adam Robson and Hughie McLeod?

'We had two major problems. We had never practised before as a seven and, in Gordon Waddell and myself, we had two stand-offs. Initially, I volunteered to play at scrum-half but Gordon said there was no way he was going to play stand-off with my service. We eventually took to the field with the following seven: Ronnie Thomson was on the wing. He was an international quarter-miler and had represented Scotland in the Commonwealth Games. He had real pace and stamina. Alan Godson played centre, a gifted ball player who was an elusive runner, but eccentric at times. Gordon Waddell and I were at half-back and he proved to be a revelation at scrum-half. Cameron Boyle used his height and strength to win line-out ball and scrummage at tight-head prop. Mike Weston from the West country, who won three blues, was a mobile hooker, and John Brash was the swashbuckling wing forward. For younger readers, he was very much in the Neil Back mould.

'I suppose we upset the odds by defeating Hawick but tries by Gordon Waddell, Alan Godson and myself secured a 13–8 first-round win. We were surprised to beat Stewarts FP so easily in the second round, but Melrose were a real handful in the semi-final. Melrose opened the scoring against us when Wattie Hart went over. A Davie Chisholm penalty extended the Rose lead to six points but an Alan Godson try which I managed to convert reduced the deficit to one point. However, Alex Hastie restored their lead and a Chisholm conversion took the half-time score to 11–5. Early second-half tries by John Brash and Gordon Waddell took the score to 15–11 but Alex Hastie popped up from nowhere to score for Melrose. As Melrose pressed for a final score, roared on by the crowd, Cameron Boyle silenced the Greenyards faithful by racing home from our own 25.

'Although the final turned out to be rather one-sided, it was a tremendous moment for my father because my younger brother Ronnie was playing scrum-half for Heriots and he had watched his sons play in seven out of the 15 ties. Between us, we had scored 61 points. Not a bad day out for the Scotland family.'

Having lost in the final at Murrayfield the previous Saturday, Royal High School went one better at Melrose in 1961 by defeating Heriots FP in a closely contested final. Although they were not one of the fancied sides, Jack Dunn, writing in the *Scotsman* on the Saturday morning of the Sevens, proclaimed: 'stranger things could happen than that Royal High School FP might create a flutter'. After convincing wins over Gala, Edinburgh Wanderers and Melrose they defeated Heriots FP in the final by 12–10. Jim Lacey opened the scoring with an immaculate penalty goal from the touchline. This was followed by a try from J. Blake who, with Lacey, proved to be outstanding tacklers for the 'School'. J.M.K. Weir scored for Heriots and R.J. Scotland added a further two points. The try of the afternoon was scored by Royal High skipper Pringle Fisher when he leapt like a salmon to catch a J.A. Nichol cross kick. What else would you expect from a basketball international?

In the second half, Royal High were reduced to six men when Nichol limped off to the wing. Davie Edwards, who had missed the 1960 final due to injury, pulled a try back for Heriots but Lacey saved the day for Royal High when he thumped the ball into touch and referee G.K. Rome blew the final whistle.

London Scottish, who first appeared at the Melrose Sevens in 1935, finally triumphed in 1962 at the tenth attempt. R.H. Thomson and A.C.W. Boyle, who had collected winners' medals with Cambridge University in 1960, were in the starting line-up but it was half-backs I.H.P. Laughland and J.A.T. Rodd who caught the eye. Both London Scottish and Hawick had secured a comfortable passage to the final. The large crowd were eagerly anticipating the clash between the exiles and the Robbie Dyes. Stevie got the Hawick contingent roaring when he sneaked in for a blind-side try, but a blistering turn of pace allowed R.H. Thomson to retaliate for the Anglos and a Boyle conversion put them ahead.

G.H. Willison, a late replacement for H.F. McLeod, converted another Stevenson try before going over in the corner to give the greens a half-time lead of 11–5. Thomson raced past the Hawick defence to narrow the gap and the trusty boot of Boyle added the finishing touch. With the home crowd whistling for time, I.H.P. Laughland ran from his own 25 to put London Scottish ahead and, with the last kick of the afternoon, Boyle promptly put over his eighth conversion to make the final score 15–11.

The 1963 tournament started with perfect conditions but midway through the afternoon torrential rain and hail fell, reducing the Greenyards pitch to a quagmire. Boroughmuir, in only their sixth visit to Melrose, created something of a surprise when they defeated Glasgow Academicals, Watsonians, Stewarts FP and Hawick to take the cup for the first time. The tie of the tournament was the nail-biting semi-final between Hawick and London Scottish which was a repeat of the 1962 final. It took seven minutes of extra time for R.G. Turnbull of Hawick to break the deadlock. However, Hawick were to taste their second successive final defeat, this time at the hands of Boroughmuir by 13–3.

In 1964 A.A. Carson became the first Gala player to pick up two Melrose medals, and one of the happiest spectators was J.H. Ferguson who had led Gala to victory in 1932. Yet it could have been so different. In their first-round tie against Edinburgh Accies, Gala were cruising to a 13–3 win with two minutes to go. Defensive blunders allowed the Accies to score three tries. With the score at 13–12, J.D. Jardine saw his conversion attempt hit the post and Gala weathered the storm. Convincing victories against holders Boroughmuir and Stewarts FP set up the final most of the crowd had been anticipating – Gala v. London Scottish. If you ever venture into the Auld Mill in Galashiels on a Saturday night, some of the old-timers will tell you that this was one of the best ever Melrose finals.

One of the fascinating personal duels was at scrum-half, with D.S. Paterson, 'The Young Pretender', against J.A.T. Rodd, the current Scotland scrum-half. Although Dunc won the battle that day, it would be another five years before he wore the Scotland number nine shirt. The lead changed hands no fewer than four times, and at 9–8 for Gala it was still anyone's game. A.S. Amos, the Gala centre, had different ideas. He sold a great dummy on the half-way line and ran half the length of the field to score. J.W.C. Turner's conversion then put the final out of reach for the Anglos. Missing from the London Scottish starting line-up that day was I.H.P. Laughland. He would return.

Memory Match I.H.P. Laughland, London Scottish, 1965

I.H.P. Laughland was first capped by Scotland in 1959 and gained the last of his 31 caps in 1967. He is best remembered as the mastermind behind a magnificent London Scottish Seven who won at both Melrose and Middlesex in the same year. A natural ball player, he would have been successful at any sport he played. When he retired from rugby he took up golf and was soon down to a three-handicap. He once played football in a Scottish Cup-tie for Nairn County and turned down the opportunity to have trials with Celtic.

'It was a great time to play for London Scottish. Most of us were young and single and our social life revolved round rugby. We also had some very talented players at that time. Ronnie Thomson, Ken Scotland, John Brash and Cameron Boyle had joined us from a successful Cambridge side and our backs and forwards were full of internationals.

'We are often given credit, or take the blame, for changing the way in which seven-a-side rugby is played, but I like to think that the Fijians have modelled their play on the London Scottish way. A great deal has been talked and written about this but the idea is quite simple. Ken Scotland came up with the idea. In order to play effective seven-a-side rugby, you must retain possession and run off the ball. A similar tactic was adopted by the Arthur Rowe inspired Tottenham Hotspur side of the 1950s. It was known as push and run. Although we had some naturally talented footballers, the reason why we won so many tournaments was that we practised harder than anyone else.

'When the clocks changed, we were able to train in Hyde Park about four nights a week. The first half-hour would be spent on fitness training, but we always had a ball in our hands. How often do you see a winger throw the ball away in a tie? It is because he spends his life receiving passes, never giving them. We would think nothing of trying a line-out move 100 times until we got it right. Sandy Lyle did not win the Masters with his bunker shot up the 18th. He won it because he had hit 5,000 similar shots in practice rounds.

'Ronnie Thomson was invaluable for fitness training. We were taught to relax in our running after we had made the initial break, with the result that most people in our team could score from 50 yards out.

'We were on the second tie against Edinburgh Accies, whom we beat 11–0, and we managed to score four tries against Jedforest before reaching the semi-final. We expected to meet the Barbarians at some stage but Kelso pulled off quite a shock in the second round. The four English caps in the Barbarians line-up were not amused. Our semi-final against Stewarts was a close-run affair. I always enjoyed my tussles with Gregor Sharp, and in Sandy Hinshelwood they had a winger who was later to become a team-mate.

'The final was a repeat of the 1962 tournament when we met Hawick in the final. Tremayne, who had largely allowed those of us outside him to do the work prior to the final, came into his own and broke from our own 25 before handing over to Brash to Shackleton to Hodgson for Laughland to convert. We scored again following a scrum on the Hawick line, but Dave Cranston intercepted my pass behind my own line and duly converted. We goofed again when Shack failed to hold the ball and Peter Robertson pounced to score. Cranston then levelled the scores. However, the spring evenings in Hyde Park began to tell. Shack and John Brash scored two further tries to make it 16–10.'

London Scottish came back in 1966 to defend their title but they had inadvertently left the cup in London and the Melrose Committee had to bring out the original Ladies Cup. The host side had delighted the crowd by knocking out the holders 11–10 in the semi-final, turning round a ten-point defeat. After winning at Gala the previous Saturday, a powerful Hawick Seven had swept into the final without conceding a point and, as a contest, the final was over

Hawick, winners of the Spring Sevens Grand Slam, 1966

in three minutes. H. Whitaker broke round the blind side for the first try. A. Graham and R.W. Brydon were next on the score sheet.

Hawick conceded points for the first time in the tournament when J. Blacklock scored a consolation try. In the second half three C.M. Telfer tries put Hawick out of reach before Blacklock scored his second try for Melrose. This Hawick Seven would be around for some time to come. If Alastair Frater was the best uncapped centre of the 1950s, Harry Whitaker was the best uncapped scrum-half of the 1960s.

Memory Match R.B. Welsh, Hawick, 1967

The 1966–67 season witnessed the pinnacle of Rob Welsh's rugby career. The Hawick centre won his first cap against Ireland and was a member of the all-conquering Hawick Seven who won the complete Spring and Autumn Border circuit in 1966 and, by winning the Spring Gala and Melrose tournaments, they won a remarkable ten in a row. Along with Colin Telfer and Peter Robertson, Welsh played in all ten finals.

'It all started at Gala in the spring of 1966. When the Hawick selectors announced the Hawick Seven, there was uproar in the town. Colin Telfer, who had played at Melrose between the semi-final and the final for Royal High School the previous year, was still in short trousers, and what were they playing prop forwards at sevens for?

'Clubs had no recognised coaches in those days but Robin Charters must take a lot of the credit for our success. The feeling in the town made us even more determined and we spent Tuesday and Thursday nights practising the basics. A total of 11 players played in those ten finals and the reason we were able to have the continuity was that we stuck to the same basic game plan: win the ball from the kick-off, move it out to the wing as quickly as possible and, if an overlap did not exist, move the ball back inside. As well as having great knowledge about the game, Robin was also a great man-manager. After a fairly tight second-round tussle with Royal High School and a place in the semi-final secured, I was sitting down with Peter Robertson and Harry Whitaker when Robin walked in and read the riot act. A few minutes later, Colin Telfer came in and it was all smiles and pats on the back.

'I don't want to take anything away from the Gala side of the early 1970s, but when we won our Grand Slam we faced some very good sides. Although they never played at Melrose, Cardiff

Training College played at both Gala and Kelso and, in our tie against them at Poynder Park, Harry Whitaker made Gareth Edwards look a very ordinary scrum-half.

'Looking back, it was exciting at the time but by keeping on winning we were putting ourselves under a lot of pressure. By the time the 1967 tournaments had started, everyone bar the Hawick supporters wanted us to lose.

'In our semi-final against London Scottish, Sandy Hinshelwood could have been a threat but our forwards never let him have the ball and Alex Jackson, who had replaced his brother Doug, ended up our top points scorer. Our forwards were accused of being too small and not being mobile but nobody took the ball from them. We faced Kelso in the final, who beat us at Hawick the following week, and Harry was in brilliant form in the final with two of his famous blind-side runs. Why did the run end at Hawick? I'm not making excuses but some of us went to South Africa that summer with the Scottish Border Club and we had to have jags between Melrose and Hawick Sevens. In many ways, it was a relief when we were finally beaten.'

The 1968 tournament was won by Loughborough Colleges, who had taken the sevens game to a new plateau. It was also to be the year when the last rugby-special trains chugged into Melrose. By the following January, the government had pulled the plug on the old Waverley line in one of the greatest acts of political vandalism inflicted on the Scottish Borders. R.L. Barlow, G.A.C. Sellar and D. Shaw were fine forwards for the students and would not have looked out of place in any back division. Outside Winship at scrum-half, the Colleges had two real flyers and in Keith Fielding they had the player of the tournament. A. Robinson, the linkman and goal-kicker, helped himself to no fewer than 17 conversions that afternoon. Easy wins over Edinburgh Wanderers and Langholm took Loughborough into the semi-final against Hawick, who were the only team to give them any competition. Even then, the pace of Fielding was too much for the Robbie Dyes. Royal High School emerged as the surprise packet of the top half of the draw, defeating Melrose 11–8 after extra time. In a one-sided final, Fielding scored before Royal High School had touched the ball. Three further tries all goaled by Robinson before half-time took the result beyond reach of Royal High and the Leicestershire side finished comfortable winners by 30–5.

In a remarkable reversal of fortunes, Loughborough Colleges achieved back-to-back victories at Melrose in 1969 despite losing the Gala final by 38–5 to Gala. The students had the luxury of being up in the Borders between the Gala and Melrose Sevens and were tactically more aware than the Braw Lads. D.S. Paterson, who had masterminded Gala the previous week, was not allowed the freedom he had enjoyed, and Drew Gill and John Frame were closely marked. The outstanding tie of the day was the second semi-final between Gala and London Scottish, who had two Scottish internationals in their line-up in S. Wilson and A.F. McHarg. A penalty goal in extra time put Gala into the final by 13–10. The Colleges, with one change from the side which had won the previous year with D. Cooke replacing Fielding, were too strong for Gala but a strong, blustering wind and a lively ball meant that the standard of rugby was not as good as in their first win.

THE 1970s

Apart from the magnificent Gala Seven who won three times on the trot between 1970 and 1972, honours at Melrose during the 1970s were shared equally between the Border and Edinburgh clubs. Television coverage brought an added dimension by attracting new spectators to the sport, and this was a time when each team seemed to have their own personality.

Andy Irvine of Heriots, Peter Brown of Gala, Jim Renwick of Hawick, Alan Lawson of Edinburgh Wanderers, Roy Laidlaw of Jedforest, Keith Robertson of Melrose, Douglas Morgan of Stewarts/ Melville, Andrew Ker of Kelso, John Rutherford of Selkirk and Bruce Hay of Boroughmuir were just a few of the household names who contributed so much to the Melrose Sevens during the 1970s. The fact that honours were spread evenly during this time made it a great spectator sport because very few people were able to predict the eventual winners. It was also a time when teams fielded all their international stars – a time before players went on end-of-season tours every year.

Although Loughborough Colleges and London Scottish were popular visitors during the 1960s, no guest side would win a Melrose tournament until the 1983 centenary event.

A number of prestigious English and Welsh club sides came up to Melrose, including St Luke's College, Loughborough Colleges, Bridgend, Yorkshire Wanderers, Rosslyn Park, Public School Wanderers and Richmond, but none of them were successful. This led to the suggestion that bringing these sides to Melrose was a waste of money, and that their places should go to Scottish clubs. With the possible exception of Bridgend, who fielded a much-changed side from the one published in the 1972 programme, all the other clubs came up to Melrose with the intention of winning. Rosslyn Park had won countless seven-a-side tournaments in England, but the truth of the matter was that they just were not good enough to win Melrose at that time. Besides, the bulk of the spectators who came to Melrose actually wanted to see the guest sides lose. The Melrose Committee were in a no-win situation.

Memory Match A. Brown, Gala, 1970

Arthur 'Hovis' Brown won the first of his five Melrose medals in 1970 and was part of the magnificent Gala Seven who swept the Border Sevens circuit in the early 1970s. He was capped five times for Scotland as a full-back but formed a formidable half-back partnership with Dunc Paterson in the Gala Seven. With a cheeky grin and an infectious enthusiasm for rugby, he remains one of the most popular figures in the game.

'Your first Melrose Medal is always something special and the 1970 final was a repeat of the previous year. Loughborough Colleges were a great side at that time, but I think we showed them too much respect in the 1969 final.

'We were on the second tie against Royal High and were losing 10–9. P.C. [Brown] dived over and, after his unsuccessful conversion attempt, the referee blew for full-time. That was the thing about P.C., you never knew what he was going to do next. At Gala the previous week, when we had won our own Sports, P.C. had kicked 11 out of 15 conversions. At Melrose it was nothing out of 11. We were a well-balanced side with P.C. and Kenny Oliver winning possession at the line-out and Johnny Brown striking at the scrums.

*The Magnificent
Seven – Gala, 1972*

Dunc was the general behind the scrum but he let Drew Gill, John Frame and myself do all the running in the early ties and saved himself for the semi-final and final.

'We beat West of Scotland and St Luke's quite easily to reach the final. We were tactically more astute that year. Dunc played as a sweeper to cover the kick ahead and Drew Gill was to stick tight on Keith Fielding. In the first few minutes, Fielding broke clear but Drew Gill caught him and brought off a great tackle. We regained possession and Drew Gill scored after escaping Fielding's tackle. Dunc did a goalie dive to prevent Loughborough from scoring, then regained his balance, picked up the ball and took a return pass to score on the corner. Fielding fumbled for Drew Gill to score another and then P.C. raced in from the 25. We could then relax and enjoy the rest of the final. That night we went off to the Hydro for a few celebratory drinks. I cannot remember much after that.'

The following year Gala returned to successfully defend their title but Borders and Scottish rugby followers were shocked when Jock Turner, at the age of 27, announced that this would be his last game of rugby. After disposing of Langholm and Royal High School, Gala faced a difficult semi-final against an A.R. Irvine inspired Heriots side. Trailing by 14–8 with three minutes to go, D.S. Paterson scored in front of the posts for P.C. Brown to convert. From the resulting kick-off, P.C. knocked on and all Heriots needed to do was retain possession. Johnny Brown took a vital strike against the head and J.W.C. Turner raced in for the winning try. In a one-sided final, Hawick were no match for Gala, with K. Hendrie, a late replacement for J.N.M. Frame, grabbing a brace of tries. P.C. Brown scored the try of the day with an outrageous dummy, holding the ball in typical P.C. basketball style.

Gala became the first club to win the Melrose Sevens three times in a row since Heriots in 1940, making them the undisputed Sevens champions of this era. The 1972 victory was also a personal milestone for Gala scrum-half Dunc Paterson, who was collecting his 50th Border Sevens medal. It was achieved by the same seven who had won at Melrose two years earlier.

It was a particularly satisfying afternoon for the Gala scrum-half. Waiting to face Gala in the final were Edinburgh Wanderers, who

The second Saturday in April, the Greenyards, Melrose

Keith Robertson surrounded by autograph-hunters

Local rivals Melrose and Hawick in an early round tussle

The French Barbarians in party mood

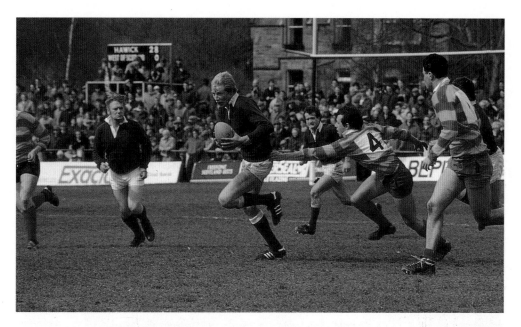

The Robbie Dyes power their way to the next round

'Get the ball out wide, there's an overlap!'

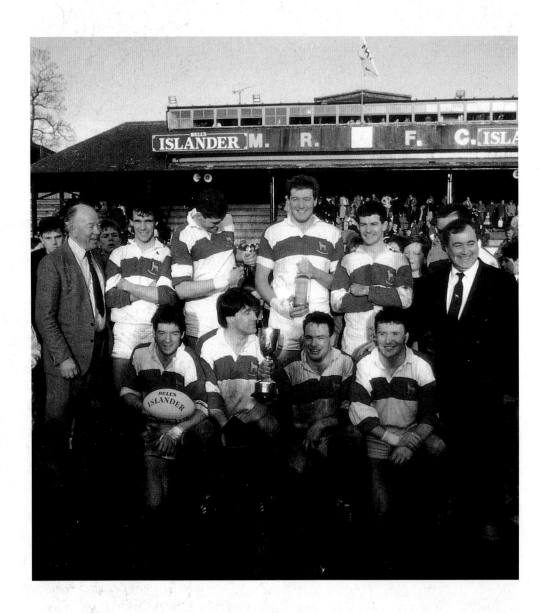

When Irish eyes are smiling: the Irish Wolfhounds

It didn't take Bay of Plenty long to find their way around the Greenyards

A packed crowd enjoy the Centenary Sevens in 1983

Jethart's here – they were in 1974

*Stewarts/Melville –
winners, 1979*

were rapidly emerging as fine exponents of the seven-a-side game. A.J.M. Lawson had just replaced D.S. Paterson as Scotland's scrum-half, but it was the old master who was to come out ahead of 'The Young Pretender' on this occasion with a 28–10 win in the final. This was probably the Gala Seven at their peak. What a tragedy that they were not invited to the Middlesex Sevens that year. Scotland's representatives were West of Scotland, who had lost their first tie at Melrose by 28–0 to Loughborough Colleges.

The 1973 tournament will be remembered as the one at which the longest kick in the history of rugby football was recorded. Playing for Kelso in a second-round tie against Watsonians, George Fairbairn's conversion attempt sailed between the posts and landed in a passing lorry. Would the owner of the vehicle please return the ball to Melrose RFC.

In the same year, Edinburgh Wanderers were to record their first Border tournament victory after losing a number of finals since 1969. In their early ties, the Wanderers had clocked up the points, scoring 72 points against Glasgow Academicals, Heriots and Kelso. The scoreline of 16–10 against Rosslyn Park suggests a closely contested final, but Wanderers had raced into a 16–0 lead with R. Proudfoot and A. Lawson dictating the play at half-back. D. Sellar, who had enjoyed previous success with Loughborough Colleges, was the outstanding forward on view. Taking charge of his last final as a whistler was J. Dun of Melrose after 13 years as the man in the middle.

1974 was the year of the underdog with seeded sides crashing out of the tournament. Edinburgh Wanderers, the holders and winners of the Murrayfield Sevens, lost to a Melrose side after extra time. Making his début for Melrose was K.W. Robertson. Kelso, winners at Netherdale, were shocked by Glasgow High and finalists Stewarts/Melville dispatched Loughborough Colleges by 26–6. Jedforest were to win the trophy this year for the first time since 1904 and were the sole Borders side left in the competition at the semi-final stage. With the crowd roaring for a Jed victory, skipper G.W. Turnbull did not disappoint the large gallery. Two tries by him and two by Robbie Lindores took Jed to a 22–0 interval lead. D. Morgan scored a consolation try for Stewarts/Melville, but Jedforest had won by 32–6.

Melrose won their own Sports in 1975, a feat which had not been

Melrose – winners,
1975

achieved since 1952. Watching over events that day was Charlie Drummond, President of the Scottish Rugby Union, who had picked up his one and only Melrose Medal a quarter of a century earlier. Six out of the seven Melrose players came out of Gala Academy; the other was St Boswells boy and Kelso High-educated K.W. Robertson. With the television cameras at the Greenyards that day, Robertson was given the platform to display his dazzling skills as a centre. Apart from having enormous natural talent, Keithy possessed an amazing will to win and was undoubtedly the most dedicated player of his generation. In a first-class career spanning almost 20 years, barring injuries and representative call-ups, you could count on one hand the number of Tuesday and Thursday evening training sessions he missed at the Greenyards.

All four Melrose games were tight and they needed a last-minute try from Rob Moffat to win their first-round tie with Stewarts/Melville FP. Richmond proved to be equally difficult second-round opponents and it took the footballing skills of 'veteran of the team' Kenny Dodds to secure a semi-final place. Their closest match was against Edinburgh Wanderers but two tries from K.W. Robertson saw them make the final. Gala took the lead in the final against a young Melrose side with Carruthers and Gill scoring, but the turning point in the game came when Robin Wood intercepted a Carruthers pass to score from midfield. Jim Henderson kicked past A.R. Brown and won the race to the touchdown before two vintage Robertson tries in the second half took Melrose to a 22–14 victory.

Boroughmuir created something of a record in 1976 when they amassed a staggering 122 points in four ties. Two borderers, D. Wilson, ex-Melrose, and G. Hogg, ex-Hawick, played a prominent part in the Boroughmuir success. In the semi-final, a fascinating confrontation took place between Bruce Hay and Andy Irvine with the 'Muir man on top on this occasion. Both full-backs for their respective clubs in the 15-a-side game, it was normally Irvine who would be picked at number 15 with Hay winning several of his caps as a winger. The other semi-final was a real battle between the previous year's winners, Melrose, and Stewarts/Melville FP. It took seven minutes of extra time before A.W. Blackwood gathered a kick ahead and sprinted for the line. This bruising encounter took its toll on Stewarts/Melville and the final was one-way traffic. Boroughmuir cruised to a 22–0 interval lead, eventually winning by 32–10.

The 1977 tournament was unique in two ways. Firstly, Melrose Rugby Club were celebrating their centenary and secondly, the Sevens were now being sponsored by the Northern Rock Building Society. Even rugby supporters were having to pay for the loan Chancellor James Callaghan borrowed from the International Monetary Fund. The 1977 programme had doubled in price to 20 pence. Despite all these happenings behind the scenes, this was a scrappy affair, with Gala the best of a number of ordinary-looking sides. J. Berthinussen excelled for Gala in the loose with D. Millar and A. Brown providing the jinking runs at half-back. Every member of the Gala squad scored that day, with Colin Gass helping himself to two tries in the final after replacing D. Carruthers. In a repeat of the 1975 final, Gala turned the tables on Melrose, defeating the host side by 30–10.

In 1978 Kelso became the fifth Border club to collect a Melrose Sevens victory, which was eagerly anticipated in their home town. The late Matt Ballantyne had bequeathed a black box to Kelso Rugby Club which was not to be opened until Kelso had won a Melrose final. Returning to Kelso that evening, the Kelso players could hardly contain themselves. The box was eventually opened and inside there was an old threepenny bit.

The 1977–78 season will go down as one of Kelso's best ever. They had just won the Second Division title of the National League, Kelso A had won the Border Junior League and Kelso Harlequins the semi-junior title. Seventeen-year-old Roger Baird and 18-year-old team-mate Bob Hogarth led the way, finishing joint top scorers at Melrose.

Along with Langholm, Selkirk are the only Border club not to have won at Melrose and their cause was not helped this year when the referee tripped up Billy Rutherford, younger brother of John, leaving Gala's Ken Lawrie the simplest of tasks to pick up the ball and score.

The previous Saturday, Stewarts/Melville had knocked Kelso out in the first round at Gala by 16–12 but in the final at Melrose, Kelso cruised to a 16–0 lead with Andrew Ker, the veteran of the Kelso side at 23, giving the ball to the Kelso teenage back division at the right moment.

Guest side Richmond had looked impressive in their early ties but against a workmanlike Kelso side they were crushed 26–6 in the semi-final and Stewarts/Melville suffered a similar fate in the final, going down 22–4.

Stewarts/Melville eventually won a tournament at Melrose in 1979 despite the handicap of losing Douglas Morgan in a first-round tie against West of Scotland. Three Border clubs – Hawick, Kelso and Gala – had reached the semi-finals, but in a repeat of last year's final it was the City side who would emerge as victors.

It was in the forwards where Stewarts/Melville gained the upper hand, with the Brewster brothers and Jim Calder getting the better of Paxton, Callander and Hewit. This allowed Blackwood and Forsyth the possession they needed and Roger Baird, the Kelso youngster, spent the final chasing Blackwood, although he did score twice in the second half. For Ian Forsyth, it was a case of 14th-time lucky. He first appeared for Stewarts in 1965, playing in four finals before winning that elusive medal.

THE 1980s

For Melrose Sevens supporters, debate will continue as to who were the best seven ever to play at Melrose. For sheer consistency, it is unlikely that any team will match the feat achieved by Kelso between 1978 and 1992, appearing in 13 Melrose finals out of a possible 15. Even in their barren years, 1983 and 1987, Kelso reached the semi-final. During the 1980s, Kelso won the cup six times and were runners-up twice. Guest teams were brought in from England, Wales, the United States, Hong Kong and France, but on most occasions the cup made the short trip down the River Tweed.

One of the strengths of the Kelso side was that they never had a weak link, but one interesting statistic worthy of note is that during the time Kelso reigned supreme on the Border Sevens Circuit, winning over 80 tournaments, they never won a cup when Andrew Ker did not play. The Kelso stand-off was one of the greatest playmakers of all time. Although he defied the golden rule of sevens by kicking away possession, how often was there a Baird or a Common on the end of one of those downfield punts? However, like all great sevens, Kelso were fortunate to have an outstanding scrum-half, Bob Hogarth, the most important position in the seven-a-side game. He always seemed to reserve his best form for Melrose, and Andrew Ker is the first to acknowledge how much he benefited from playing outside his half-back partner.

Kelso's success in 1986 was probably their best performance, defeating two star-studded guest sides and, in doing so, emulating Gala's feat of the 1970s by winning three tournaments on the bounce. With an international forward trio of Eric Paxton, Gary Callender and John Jeffrey, Kelso simply denied the opposition with that vital ingredient for sevens rugby: possession.

During the early 1980s, Stewarts/Melville were perhaps the only team which could give Kelso a stern test, but in the first round of the 1980 competition they were surprisingly beaten by Edinburgh Accies 12–10. That year, Stewarts/Melville won the three other Border Spring Sevens, but it would be Kelso who would collect the greatest prize.

The surprising defeat of Stewarts/Melville had allowed Melrose a relatively easy access to the final, with the St Boswells pair Keith Robertson and Colin Ruthven showing their paces. Kelso had also progressed to the final without much difficulty and after their defeat of London Scottish by 20–4 we were all set for a Border final. Although Melrose took the lead, it did not take long for the Tweedsiders to get into top gear and with the help of a penalty try they eased to a 24–4 lead. For Kelso, Bob Hogarth did most of the damage, ending the day with a haul of 44 points from six tries and ten conversions.

Winning the Melrose Sevens in 1981 capped a great season for the Gala club who had already won the Scottish Championship and the Border League. It was also a remarkable personal achievement for Arthur Brown who had come in as a late replacement for D. Bryson at scrum-half and picked up his fifth Melrose Medal. However, it could have been so different. Gala struggled to beat Watsonians 16–14 in the first tie of the day. In the second round, they escaped from jail against Melrose. At the end of full-time the score was 12-all with Melrose having scored three tries to Gala's two. Vital conversion attempts were missed by Melrose, including one in front of the posts. Into extra time, Gala winger Peter Dods escaped the clutches of Robertson and Gala were into the semi-finals. These were contested by four Border clubs – Gala, Hawick, Kelso and Selkirk, with Gala and Kelso reaching the final. The highlight of the last match of the day was a thundering tackle from Derek White on Eric Paxton a few feet from the Gala line. Dods picked up the loose ball and ran the length of the field to score. Gordon Dickson, another late replacement, was on the score sheet as Gala cruised to a 26–10 victory.

Returning to the Greenyards in 1982 for their fifth visit since 1951, much was expected of Middlesex holders Rosslyn Park who had England internationalist Andy Ripley in their ranks. However, as so many guest teams have discovered over the years, a trip to

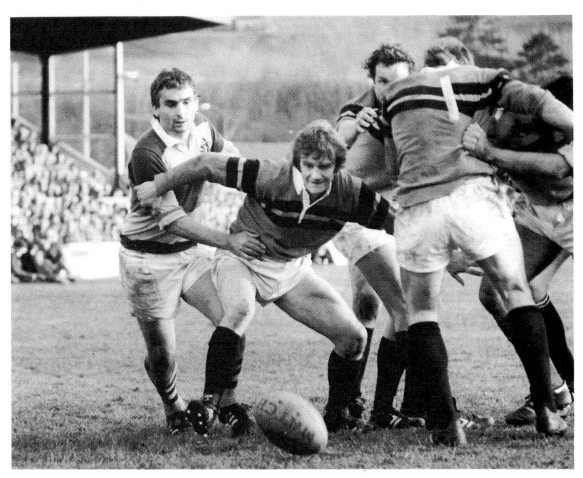

Douglas Morgan of Stewarts/Melville ready to pounce against the French Barbarians

Melrose is not for the faint-hearted and they were knocked out of their stride by a young Melrose side with Newtown St Boswells youngster David 'Scrog' Shiel making his début at scrum-half. In the other half of the draw, Kelso were making heavy work of things, narrowly beating Gala in the second round and requiring extra time to dispose of Watsonians in the semi-final. After their giant-killing against Rosslyn Park, Melrose fell to Heriots in the semi-final by 12–6. In one of the highest-scoring finals in recent years, Heriots, without Andy Irvine, scored five tries in the first half. Playing Kelso at their own game, Peter Hewitt kicked ahead and the ball bounced into his lap for a try. Powerful Scottish winger Bill Gammell added two more tries and, with a winning margin of 40–16, the cup returned to Goldenacre for the first time since 1958.

On Saturday, 9 April 1983, Melrose Rugby Football Club celebrated their centenary sevens in one of the largest sporting gatherings ever to take place in the Scottish Borders. With 24 teams taking part, the tournament started at 11.30 a.m. and lasted until 7 p.m., attracting a crowd of over 16,000. Playing for the new Ladies Cup, it was a regal occasion. The cup was presented to the winners by Her Royal Highness, Princess Alice, Duchess of Gloucester, the first member of the Royal Family to attend the Melrose Sevens.

A special sevens centenary committee had been set up two years earlier and invitations had been sent out to all the Home Rugby Unions to nominate a leading club to represent their country at the tournament. In addition, it was the first time that the Barbarians and the French Barbarians had appeared on the same stage.

England promised to send the winners of the 1982 Middlesex Sevens but that posed something of a problem since the tournament was won that year by Stewarts/Melville FP. However, Richmond, who were runners-up at Twickenham, accepted the challenge for England.

The Welsh Rugby Union selected the South Glamorgan Institute, or Cardiff Training College as they were better known. South Glamorgan Institute were selected to represent Wales on account of their victory in the 1982 Welsh National Sevens.

Bangor RFC, the Ulster Senior League Champions, were chosen to represent Ireland, and Tynedale, who had the distinction of being the first English club to win the Melrose Sports in 1886, made up the sixth guest side.

*The victorious
French Barbarians
after the final
whistle*

Given the track record of guest sides at Melrose, two teams reaching the semi-final would have pleased the organisers. The first shock of the day took place when unfavoured Royal High School defeated the Barbarians in the first round by 14–12. With five internationalists in their ranks, including new England backs supremo Les Cusworth, the Babas were caught cold. It took two late tries by the French Barbarians to win their first-round encounter against Watsonians by 18–12. The Frenchmen improved with every tie, defeating Glasgow High/Kelvinside and Heriots before running up 30 points against Richmond in the semi-final. In the other semi-final, Kelso and Stewarts/Melville locked horns again, with the City men coming out on top 18–14 courtesy of three Morgan conversions.

In the final, Stewarts/Melville drew first blood but tries from Fourniol and Andrieu put the Frenchmen ahead. The turning point in the final was when Desry charged down Morgan's hack to score for the Barbarians and, in the second half, further tries by Fourniol and J.B. Lafond brought this historic day to a close.

During the post-match celebrations a couple of Frenchmen had used their Gallic charms to get themselves invited back to the homes of two young ladies from Galashiels. Their hospitality must have been lavish because the guests kindly gave them their Melrose winners' medals. On returning to France and, realising the error of their ways, they wrote to Melrose Rugby Club to enquire whether they might be presented with another couple of medals. The answer was *non*!

Kelso returned to their winning ways in 1984, running up a staggering 142 points in four ties, with Bob Hogarth notching up a personal tally of 62. The French Barbarians, showing a much-changed side from the one which won the centenary sevens, must be one of the most expensive guest sides to have appeared at the Greenyards, going out 18–16 to Boroughmuir in the first round. Stewarts/Melville, appearing in their sixth final in 11 years, were no match for a rampant Kelso side, with captain Eric Paxton going over for hree tries in the final. It was a memorable day for the Calder family, though, with brothers Finlay, Jim and John making up the Stewarts/Melville scrum.

In 1985, the tournament became known as the British Caledonian Melrose Sevens. The sponsor's advertising slogan was 'We never forget you have a choice'. For the punter trying to select a winner there was only one choice – Kelso. Blackheath, from South London, and Bridgend were the guest sides that year but Melrose made light work of the Welshmen in the first round, winning by 22–4. Blackheath looked an accomplished side with Mick 'The Munch' Skinner making his first visit to the Greenyards, but they finally succumbed to Kelso in the semi-final. Even a first-round injury to international hooker Gary Callender failed to put Kelso off their stride. Mike Minto simply slotted into the Kelso machine. Showing superb fitness and a pathological hatred for giving away tries, Kelso ran up a total of 40 points in a Melrose final for the second successive year.

The 1986 tournament was a great success for Melrose President Tom Mitchell and his committee, with all four seeds reaching the semi-finals. The guest sides that year were out of the top drawer and all three reached the last four. The Cougars became the first American representative side to appear at the Greenyards and they can be described as the American branch of the Barbarians, embracing the same principles of style, sportsmanship and rugby fellowship. Racing Club de France are the largest sports club in Europe, with over 20,000 members participating in over 20 sports. The rugby team is one of the most powerful sections of the club and their home ground is the former international stadium Stade Colombes. Wasps came to Melrose that year on the back of wins at Middlesex and Rugby, with Mark Bailey, Huw Davies, Simon Smith, Rob Lozowski and Nick Stringer – all full English caps.

Memory Match A. Ker, Kelso, 1986

Andrew Ker made his début for Kelso at the Melrose Sevens in 1973 as a teenager. Over the next 17 years, he appeared in 11 finals and has seven Melrose Medals, a record unlikely to be surpassed. Capped by Scotland at both rugby and cricket, the George Watsons PE Master recalls his greatest triumph.

'My first Melrose Medal in 1978 gave me my greatest thrill, but the victory in 1986 was the one which gave me the greatest satisfaction. We had won the 1984 and 1985 tournaments quite easily, but our semi-final tie with Wasps and the final against Racing Club are two of the hardest sevens matches I have ever played in.

'I am often asked why Kelso managed to last as long and I think there are two reasons. Firstly, we had a great belief in ourselves as a team and we believed we would win every tournament that we played in. If we played to our full potential there was no other team who could touch us. Secondly, every so often we would have two young players coming into the seven who were hungry for success, which gave a boost to the other members of the team. When I first got into the Kelso Seven, George Fairbairn and I were the youngsters in the backs. When we won our first tournament in 1978, Roger Baird, Ewan Common and Bob Hogarth had come along. Our backs stayed the same for a few years, barring injury, but John Jeffrey replaced Jim Hewit in the forwards, which hardly weakened the side. Roger Baird, Bob Hogarth, Packie and myself were in the last Kelso side to win, in 1989, but Clive Millar and Mike Minto adapted well into the side in later years.

'I am also asked what special training we did in the weeks leading up to the sevens. The answer was nothing special. We used to play our second seven or Kelso Harlequins on a Tuesday and Thursday night. More often than not we would lose. I suppose like most sportsmen we had our superstitions. We had our favourite changing-room at Melrose and before our first tie we used to always walk round the Greenyards as a group in a clockwise direction. It was amazing to see the same people standing in the same spot year after year.

'Returning to the 1986 tournament for a moment, we beat Watsonians and Boroughmuir to reach the semi-final to face Wasps. The Middlesex Sevens holders seemed nervous in the early stages and I managed to capitalise on a mistake to score the first try. Referee Brian Anderson then awarded us a penalty try for a foul on Davie Robeson. I think we relaxed a bit too much because we allowed them to come back at us. Tries by Marcus Rose, Huw Davies and Mark Bailey put them ahead before Packie equalised to

The maestros – Kelso, 1986

send the tie into extra time. We sensed that the English side were tiring and J.J. gave us an extra-time winner.

'We had watched the Cougars in an earlier tie and were impressed by Brian Vizzard, but it was Racing Club de France we faced in the final. Bob Hogarth scored first in the final but Rousset kicked over our heads and Lafond converted. I saw a gap emerge in the French defence and Bob Hogarth's conversion put us back ahead. They came back at us with two tries but J.J. was in tremendous form and he scored twice for us in the second half, and the final ended 22–16 for us.

'I have many happy memories of Melrose but this was the hardest to win. My only regret is that we never managed to record a victory at Middlesex. A Scotland tour deprived us of our best forwards and we ended up one year playing Ewan Common at prop. We were drawn against Rosslyn Park, who had a certain Martin Offiah on the wing. The rest, as they say, is history.'

Making their début at the 1987 Sports were Harlequins, holders of the Middlesex Sevens. A club steeped in history, the Harlequin Football Club was born phoenix-like from the ashes of the demised Hampstead Football Club in 1866, when teams were generally composed of 20 players a side. A founder member of the Rugby Football Union in 1871, Harlequins have two home grounds, the Rugby Football Union International ground itself and the Stoop Memorial Ground, both situated at Twickenham. Their first two ties against Stewarts/Melville and Hawick provided Andy Harriman with a training session, romping in for tries from all over the place. Jedforest gave Harlequins their stiffest test in the semi-final but the Jedforest men eventually went down 10–4. Melrose disposed of a rather lacklustre Kelso side by 16–0 in the top half of the draw, with Newtown boys Gus Redburn and 'Scrog' Shiel to the fore.

Melrose stayed with Harlequins for the first few minutes of the final, but no one in the Melrose side had the pace to catch Andy Harriman and the Ladies Cup Trophy went south of the border for the first time since 1969. If the teams appearing on the Saturday could not prevent the cup from going south, perhaps a security man at Edinburgh Airport could.

John Moore-Gillon, Vice-President of the Harlequins Club, takes

*Sassenachs triumph
– Harlequins, 1987*

up the story: 'Edinburgh Airport saw a very tired but, justifiably, high-spirited group of Quins – after all, we had achieved a unique victory and, with it, the euphoria of becoming cup holders.

'The sheer importance of winning the Sports was further exemplified when we passed through the security control. The Ladies Cup Trophy was in my bag and it alarmed the X-ray unit.

'I was shown the monitor screen and the cup certainly looked as if it were some sort of ballistic nose cone. My explanation that it was the Melrose Trophy we had just won did not prevent the security personnel from inspecting my bag. The fact is that they had patently not believed me. After all, how could an English team remove the cup legally from Scotland? They were still shaking their heads when they allowed us through to the plane.'

Appearing in their sixth final in ten years, Kelso and Jedforest contested one of the most evenly contested finals in recent years and the first to go to extra time since 1947. Jedforest had reached the final by a resounding first-round win by 38–10 against Glasgow Accies, a second-round scrap against Melrose by 6–4 and a semi-final victory over guest side Wakefield by 16–10. Kelso had defeated Heriots and guest teams Cougars (Melrose was becoming their second home) and Public School Wanderers.

In the final, two tries for Alan Tait from Ker kicks-ahead gave Kelso an early lead but, cheered on by the neutrals in the crowd, Gregor McKechnie reduced the deficit. In the second half it was Kelso who were forced to soak up Jed pressure but, on at least two occasions, overlaps were spurned. The Jed cause was not helped when Robbie Lindores had to leave the field to be replaced by a back, B. Hughes. However, constant Jed pressure eventually paid off and P. Douglas scored and a McKechnie goal took the final into extra time. A superb covering tackle by Roy Laidlaw prevented a certain try for Kelso but from the resultant line-out Kelso scored.

Making their first appearance at Melrose, but not the Border Sevens Circuit, in 1989, were Hong Kong RFU. Established in 1953, and a founder member of the Asian Rugby Football Board, they first came to the Borders in 1973, playing at both Hawick and Jedforest Sevens. Three years later the prestigious Hong Kong Sevens was started and is now a focal point in the Hong Kong social calendar.

The bulk of the Cougars squad had just come from Hong Kong, representing the national side, the Eagles, and, under the management of Keith Seaber, were still seeking their elusive first Melrose Medal.

It did not matter where the Melrose Committee were bringing guest sides from. Kelso were to record their fifth win in six years, but they did not have it all their own way after surprise packet Ayr knocked out the Cougars and Loughborough Students. Ayr stunned Kelso by taking a 12-point lead when scrum-half Bobby Gilmour burst clear for two tries. Baird pulled a try back for Kelso but P. Manning, the Ayr centre, outpaced Bob Hogarth for a third Ayr score before Robeson replied for Kelso. A kick-and-chase by – you've guessed it – A. Ker, levelled the score at 16-all. Ayr took the lead again when D. Stark outpaced the Kelso defence but the Tweedsiders' never-say-die team spirit pulled them through again when Clive Millar powered over for two tries. Kelso had won a pulsating final by 28–22.

THE 1990s

If the 1980s had left star-studded guest sides with egg on their faces, visitors to the Greenyards in the 1990s showed Border folk a thing or two about how sevens should be played.

Even by Melrose standards, the Committee pulled off a coup in 1990 by attracting Randwick, the first club from Australia to appear at Melrose. Randwick play their rugby in one of the most competitive leagues in world rugby. They play in the 12-club Sydney First Division where a club plays each of its opponents twice a season, on a home-and-away basis. Over the past 20 years Randwick had been league champions on 14 occasions. Rugby is big business in Sydney. On an average Saturday, Randwick have 11 teams on the go with annual bar takings in excess of £500,000.

For their trip to Melrose, Randwick selected a blend of youth and experience which included two world-class backs in Mark Ella and David Campese. John Maxwell, who had represented the Australian National Sevens team on six occasions, skippered the side. Of the remaining players, two had represented New South Wales. The party were led by John Howard OAM, the Randwick Club President, one of the world's outstanding rugby administrators.

Racing Club de France, who first appeared at Melrose in 1986, were the second overseas guest team but late call-offs from Jean Baptiste Lafond and Franck Mesnel left the French side under-strength and they fell at the first hurdle to Stewarts/Melville FP.

Harlequins and London Scottish filled the two remaining guest spots with current Scotland captain Gavin Hastings appearing for the exiles.

Although the centenary sevens had taken place in 1983, Saturday, 14 April 1990 was the 100th playing of the Melrose

Keith Robertson scores against Harlequins, 1990

Sevens, which attracted a record 17,000 people. Making his second appearance at Melrose that year was Welsh referee Clive Norling, regarded as one of the leading referees of his generation. Making his last appearance at Melrose Sevens was Keith Robertson, who was so close to ending his career in glory.

The 1990 tournament had been extended to 20 teams and the first-round tie between Jedforest and Stirling County kicked off at 1 p.m. precisely. Harlequins caught the eye during the early stages of the tournament, with British Lions W. Carling and P. Winterbottom in sparkling form. However, the much-fancied Londoners received a shock in the quarter-final when they faced the host side, Melrose. Robertson was in majestic form and the two sides were tied at 12-all when the game went into extra time. Melrose were awarded a penalty and the crowd watched in silence as Craig Chalmers cooly slotted over the goal. Randwick had eased their way into the semi-final with comfortable wins over Glasgow Accies and Edinburgh

Nuiquila of Randwick gives Purves of Melrose the slip

David Campese: simply the best

Accies. At the top half of the draw Kelso had won three ties to set up an all-Border semi-final against Hawick.

The Randwick v. Melrose semi-final was one of the most exciting matches ever seen at the Greenyards. With hindsight, it should have been the final. It was a privilege to watch two of the greatest entertainers in world rugby, Keith Robertson and David Campese, go through their repertoire of tricks. Just as he had done in the previous round, Chalmers kicked a penalty to put Melrose 15–12 ahead with the seconds ticking away. The Australians were awarded a penalty and, in a desperate last-gasp attempt, the ball was whisked out to Campese. Surrounded by three Melrose defenders Campo, with a lightning change of pace, made it to the corner and Randwick were in the final by the narrowest of margins, 16–15.

Kelso were no match for Randwick in the final and the Greenyards crowd were treated to some scintillating running from Campese, Ella, Walker and Nuiquila who displayed exhibition-style rugby in running up 26 points. With seven tries and eight conversions, Campese ended the day as top points scorer and leading personality. Given their outstanding record at Melrose in recent years, Kelso were rather upset that they had not been selected as one of the seeded teams, but Gala were to prove four years later that it is possible to win the Melrose Sevens after playing five ties.

By 1991, a pool system had been introduced, with each club nominating their side from a selection of ten players. Randwick returned to defend the trophy they had won in 1990, but without Campese and Ella they were a shadow of the team they were a year earlier. Yet another prestigious touring side were welcomed to the Greenyards that year: the Irish Wolfhounds with Dr Karl Mullen, captain of the 1950 British Lions tour of Australia and New Zealand, leading the party.

Kelso were given the short straw again by having to play a first-round tie but were the only Border club to reach the semi-finals. Randwick and the Irish Wolfhounds met in the top half of the draw with Kelso taking on Loughborough Students in the other semi-final. Most of the early ties had gone to form with the Irish Wolfhounds getting better with each game. Australia v. Ireland and Scotland v. England. Melrose had become a truly international

festival of rugby. A great battle emerged between the Randwick and Irish Wolfhound flyers with Brendan Hanavan just getting the better of A. Nuiquila, who had been a revelation the year before.

When Irish eyes are smiling – the Irish Wolfhounds, 1991

Kelso toiled against a hard-working Loughborough side but eventually scraped through by 16–10 to reach their 11th final since 1978. Five hard ties had taken their toll on Kelso and this time they were on the end of a drubbing. Hanavan, once again, showed his pace in the final to take the cup over the water for the first time in history.

Another milestone was achieved in 1992 when Bay of Plenty became the first New Zealand team to play in a Scottish club sevens tournament. Founded in 1911, Bay of Plenty are one of the strongest provinces in New Zealand with a strong Maori contingent. They gave the 1971 touring British Lions one of their hardest matches and in recent years have claimed the scalps of the touring Wallabies, Fiji and Western Samoa.

On the Thursday prior to sevens day, Bay of Plenty came

down to St Boswells RFC for a spot of practice against the locals. St Boswells were no slouches at sevens and had won over 20 tournaments on the junior circuit, but that evening they were given a lesson. The Kiwis scored 12 tries in about 20 minutes before retiring for an early night. Local bookmaker Dominic Forte must have had his spies down at St Boswells that night because Bay of Plenty's odds had shortened considerably by Saturday morning.

As predicted, Bay of Plenty were easing towards their prize with convincing wins over Watsonians, Gala and Hawick to reach the final in their first visit. Kelso, who had been given one of the seeded places that year, only scraped through against Jedforest and Stirling County before gaining revenge against the Irish Wolfhounds in the semi-final by 28–18. The Kiwis were just too strong for Kelso in the final but received the wrath of the 15,000 strong crowd when skipper P. Werehiko elected for a kick at goal when Bay of Plenty were 16–6 ahead. K. Irihei duly obliged after M. Jones and J. Tavini had put the New Zealanders ahead earlier in the tie. For Kelso, this was their 13th final in 15 years. Randwick, the Irish Wolfhounds and Bay of Plenty were all worthy winners, but I wonder what would have happened if they had met Andrew Ker, Bob Hogarth, John Jeffrey and Eric Paxton at their peak!

In 1993 South Africa became the last of the great southern hemisphere rugby-playing nations to have a side represented at Melrose. It was also the first invitation extended to a provincial side and Western Province took up the challenge. Sadly for South African sportsmen, two generations of rugby and cricket players have been prevented from performing on an international stage. However, Western Province have led the way by integrating the community and there are now 90 mixed-race clubs in the area.

1993 was also the year of the World Cup Sevens and internationals came from all over the world to compete for the Melrose Cup at Murrayfield. In order to help prepare a Scottish seven for this event, the Co-optimists Rugby Club were invited to send a side.

The club was founded in 1924 by rugby journalist Jock Wemyss, who was then playing for Edinburgh Wanderers, and George St Clair Murray, a rugby enthusiast who played for Watsonians. The object of the club was to promote the game of rugby football in areas where it was not the premier sport.

Considering the club has no ground, no membership fee and only one regular fixture, against East Lothian, it has a remarkable record. Players are principally chosen from Scotland but internationals from the other Home Unions have worn the famous navy-blue jersey with 'lion couchant', including Tony O'Reilly and former Welsh stand-off Jonathan Davies. During the 1984 Grand Slam season, each member of the Scottish squad played in at least one match. Their pedigree in sevens is equally impressive. In 1980 they reached the final of the Cathay Pacific Hong Kong Bank Sevens and the following year were beaten by Australia in the semi-final. In 1993, the club achieved the pinnacle of its sevens success by winning the Melrose tournament. Playing a vital part in that win was Ian Corcoran.

Memory Match I. Corcoran, Co-optimists, 1993

By the time the 1993 Melrose tournament had got under way, Ian Corcoran had spent the previous 18 months as 'Man in a Suitcase', playing rugby all over the world. In the summer of 1992 he was awarded his first cap, coming on as replacement for Kenny Milne in the second Test against Australia. The following season he was selected to play sevens in Dubai, Australia and Hong Kong. In between, he found time to lead the South of Scotland to their Scottish District Championship.

'A lot has been said about cutting down the number of overseas tours, but on a personal level, it has improved my rugby no end. A tour benefits a player in three ways. It builds up a great team spirit among the players, your level of fitness improves and playing the best players in the world raises your game.

'Although we did not win in Australia and Hong Kong, we improved as a squad and we felt confident when we returned to play at Gala. Playing as the Edinburgh Borderers we got absolutely stuffed by Gala in the final by 38–14, and you can imagine the stick I took that evening from all the Gala folk. My wife, Carrie, even presented the Gala Cup to the Gala captain.

'We stayed at the Dryburgh Abbey Hotel prior to the Melrose tournament and Douglas Morgan and John Jeffrey did a marvellous job to lift us. One defeat, even if it was a drubbing, did not make us a bad side. However, changes had to be made and having led the side on tour and at Gala, I lost the captaincy.

'Playing for the Co-optimists at Melrose, the transformation in players when they put on a dark blue jersey was amazing, and in our two opening ties we beat Stirling County and Edinburgh Accies with quite a bit to spare. This set us up against Bay of Plenty in the longest sevens second-half I have played in. Joe Tavini scored for Bay of Plenty when we were caught on the hop from a quickly taken penalty, but we were back in the hunt when David Millard went over in the corner. Gregor Townsend kicked a brilliant conversion from the touchline to put us ahead. Bay of Plenty scored again and this time the kick was converted and we were 12–7 behind. I managed to get on the score sheet in the second-half but, again, we left Gregor with a difficult kick. Sometimes players are accused of not trying to get closer to the posts when they score a try in sevens but when you have three Kiwis on your back, getting over the try line is a bonus. Gregor stroked over the conversion and we hung on for the last few minutes to win 14–12. We ran up 61 points in the final against a luckless Jed side, but they were not as bad as the score suggests. If you go more than three tries behind in sevens it is always difficult to come back as we found to our cost at Gala the previous Saturday.'

Her Royal Highness, the Princess Royal, no stranger to Scottish rugby, was a popular visitor to Melrose in 1994. Met by the Duke of Buccleuch on her arrival, she could not have chosen a worse day to come and watch rugby. In possibly the worst tournament weather ever, she braved the elements to the end to present the Ladies

The Co-optimists – winners, 1993

Centenary Cup to the winning captain.

The Co-optimists returned to defend their trophy but last year's international contingent returned to play for their club sides, and they did very well to reach the semi-final before going down to Wasps 17–10. The Londoners, current holders of the Middlesex Sevens, last appeared at Melrose in 1987 and once again assembled a strong squad.

The Australian and South African connection continued when Manly and Villager accepted invitations to play. Arch-rivals of Randwick, Manly were keen to emulate the success of their Sydney neighbours, and the crowd were looking forward to seeing Australian rugby personality Willie Ofahengue.

The Villager Club from Cape Town, South Africa, the oldest club

Michael Dods, Tom McLeish and Princess Anne brave the elements

in the country, were making their Melrose début in 1994. Used to playing on bone-hard surfaces, by the time they reached the quarter-final against Melrose the Greenyards surface was about six inches deep in mud. The host side who, over the years, have had a knack of defeating their illustrious guest sides, did it again with a pulsating 26–21 victory after extra time.

However, it was Gala who were able to adapt best to the conditions and they were to win their first Melrose Sevens since 1981. In Grant Farquharson, they had the outstanding player of the tournament with eight tries, many of which were 50-yard bursts.

In the final against Wasps, Lawrence Scrase put the Sudbury side ahead within 60 seconds, but Neil Crooks soon put Gala back on level terms. A Michael Dods conversion gave the Netherdale men a slender 7–5 interval lead. Slack play in the Gala defence allowed Simon Holmes in for a score but Dods, picking up a pass from his ankles, put the Border side back ahead. Crooks sealed victory for Gala when he held off the Wasps defence to squeeze over in the corner. Moncrieff replaced Dods for a few seconds but the Gala skipper was able to regain his composure to gratefully accept the cup from the Princess Royal.

THE CRICHTON CUP –
75 NOT OUT

Melrose Rugby Club have always been keen to promote rugby among the young players of the district for two good reasons: the enjoyment derived from playing and the recruitment of players for the future. One of the most satisfying aspects of the club winning the Scottish 15-a-side title in the 1990s is that the vast majority of the side are home grown.

Bill McLaren once described the nearest thing to heaven as 'watching Melrose Sports with his family, eating a Hawick pie'. For any youngster in the Melrose area that might read 'playing at the Greenyards, getting in the big bath and having a bottle of Middlemas lemonade and a Dalgetty pie'.

Melrose were also the pioneers of boys' sevens. In March 1892 12 teams entered a seven-a-side tournament organised by Melrose Thistle, and in 1906–07 the Trades Competition, another seven-a-side tournament, was started.

Originally, this competition seems to have been restricted to Melrose boys and not to have had any defined upper-age limit for players. However, in 1912, it was agreed that the Trades Cup be played for by boys 16 years and under and to invite a team from Newtown St Boswells.

However, it was not until the Annual General Meeting of 28 August 1920 that the minutes referred to 'The Crichton Cup' competition. During the 1914–18 war the cup was in the care of William Barrie, a grocer whose shop was towards the west end of the High Street. After the war, the organisation of the tournament was undertaken by Ralph Michie, Hamish Turner and the Secretary of Melrose RFC. By the season 1920–21, the Crichton Cup Sports arose phoenix-like out of the earlier Trades Competition.

These Sports were open to boys under the age of 16, which had been fixed in 1912. In the first year, eight districts entered teams: Central, Dingleton, Darnick, Gattonside, East Port, Newtown St Boswells, Newstead, St Boswells and Maxton.

The first tournament was won by Central and the surnames of the winning Central Seven have a familiar ring to them: H. Rutherford, S. Walker, C. Brown, E. Hart, T. Bunyan, T. Scott and D. Wilson. The youngest member of the team, Dick Wilson, was a mere ten years old. Tom Bunyan had actually been picked to play for Melrose at Langholm Sports, but a Crichton medal has more prestige than a Langholm medal. He was not the last Melrose player to turn down an appearance at Langholm. Charlie Drummond once put village before club when he chose to play for St Boswells in the Crichtons. The Sports have traditionally been played on the first Saturday in May at the Greenyards, which normally coincides with both the Langholm and the Middlesex Sevens. The Twickenham event may attract 60,000 but the Crichtons have been going longer.

In April 1929, Mr R.E. Boyd, H. McCulloch, the Club Secretary and W.J. Turner were asked to organise the competition. Mr Boyd presented a cup for junior players which was again won by Central. St Boswells A won the Crichton Cup but, because of an infringement of the rules, the cup was withdrawn. In 1936, a third cup – the Jubilee Cup – was presented by Mr J.E.S. Nisbet of Hoebridge. The ages for each section were as follows:

Boyd Cup	boys not 12 on Sports Day
Jubilee Cup	boys 12, but not 14 on Sports Day
Crichton Cup	boys not 17 on Sports Day

On Saturday, 2 May 1936, the Sports were held under these rules and the winners were:

Boyd Cup	Newtown A
Jubilee Cup	Dingleton
Crichton Cup	Central

In April 1946, the upper age limit was lowered to 'not having passed 16th birthday', but in 1947 it reverted to that fixed in 1936. In 1951 the question of presenting medals was suggested and accepted. The gate money was divided between Melrose Grammar School, Newtown St Boswells Junior Secondary and St Boswells Primary School, to be used for Sports funds. In 1973 Mr Lawrie Redpath presented a cup, the Redpath Cup for boys under the age of eight. This format has remained for the past 21 years.

In 1963, under the chairmanship of the late Johnny Johnston, father of Jimmy, it was decided to run a second tournament to be played at the King George VI Playing Fields, Newtown St Boswells, on the Saturday following the Crichton Sports. The cups played for were:

Under 17s   The Eildon Cup
Under 14s   The Hendry Cup
Under 11s   The Fiddes Cup

The Eildon Cup was presented by Johnny Ingles and was given the name because the Ingles family lived in Eildon village, a small hamlet between Melrose and Newtown St Boswells. The Hendry Cup, played for between boys of 11, 12 and 13, was donated by Ralph Michie and it is believed that Hendry was his wife's maiden name. The Fiddes Cup was given by the headmaster of Newtown St Boswells Junior Secondary School, Christopher Fiddes, and was the Crichton equivalent of the Boyd Cup. Only three members of the original committee survive: Eddie Cassie, John Murray and Douglas Cockburn. The first winners of the Eildon Cup were Newtown A and in 1964 they repeated their success in a team which included Ernie Brown, Ian 'Nathal' Murray and David 'Brick' Elliot.

By 1975 a third tournament emerged, which gave boys in the Melrose area their own Border Sevens Circuit, when St Boswells decided that they would also host a seven-a-side competition. The original event took place at St Columba's College near Dryburgh, but in recent years the tournament has been staged and organised by St Boswells Rugby Club. The St Boswells tournament has also extended invitations to the villages of Earlston and Lauder, since High School pupils in Newtown and St Boswells now go to study at Earlston rather than Kelso High School.

Four tournaments are now contested at St Boswells, with the under 17s playing for the Farmers Cup donated by former Lilliards Edge dairy farmer Thomson Eccles, who also presided at the first meeting of the St Boswells Boys Sevens. The St Boswells Trophy for under 15s was donated by St Boswells Rugby Club and the medals come out of the players' fund account. The Lessudden Cup for under 13s was given by the Lever family of St Boswells and is named after the magnificent family residence in the village. Fittingly, the under 11s competition is called the Drummond Cup, donated by the Drummond family, one of the oldest and most respected families in the village.

On 30 April 1994, the 75th anniversary of the Melrose Crichton Cup was celebrated with each player and coach receiving a special commemorative medal to mark the occasion. The Crichton Cup, originally presented by local jeweller J.D. Crichton, is still the most coveted trophy of the 11 now played for. Even the bairns who have not reached school age begin their serious Crichton training with the traditional under 5s lemonade race which takes place half-way through the afternoon. At the senior level, Scott Ruthven led St Boswells A to a hat trick of wins at Melrose, Newtown St Boswells and St Boswells. In the other eight tournaments Newtown A won five and St Boswells A won three. In other words, all competitions were won by either Newtown A or St Boswells A. Some things never change.

APPENDICES

1 Complete List of Results 1883–1930

1883

First Round
Gala 14 Selkirk 0
St Cuthberts Hawick 14 Earlston 0
Melrose 14 St Ronans Innerleithen 0
Gala Forest v. Kelso – Gala Forest wo

Semi-Final
Melrose 11 Gala Forest 0
Gala 9 St Cuthberts Hawick 0

Final
Melrose 3 Gala 0

1884

First Round
Gala 6 St Cuthberts Hawick 0
Melrose 3 Gala Union 0
Kelso v Duns – Kelso wo
Innerleithen 3 Selkirk Volunteers 0

Semi-Final
Melrose 8 Kelso 0
Gala 5 Innerleithen 0

Final
Gala 3 Melrose 0

1885

First Round
Gala 16 Gala Rovers 0
Innerleithen v. Gala Thistle – Gala Thistle wo
Gala Star 6 Ettrickbank Selkirk 0
Gala Union 3 Hawick and Wilton 0
Melrose 8 St Cuthberts Hawick 0

Second Round
Melrose 3 Gala 0

Semi-Final
Gala Union 3 Gala Star 0
Melrose 13 Gala Thistle 0

Final
Melrose 9 Gala Union 0

1886

First Round
Tynedale 17 Abbotsford 0
Melrose 10 Gala Union 0
Gala 5 St Cuthberts Hawick 3
Hawick 6 Ladhope 0

Second Round
Gala Thistle 15 Ladhope Union 0
Tynedale 17 Gala Waverley 0
Melrose 13 Hawick and Wilton 5
Hawick 3 Gala 0

Semi-Final
Tynedale 3 Gala 0
Melrose 6 Hawick 0

Final
Tynedale 6 Melrose 0

1887

First Round
Kelso 8 Gala Waverley 3
Hawick and Wilton 6 Innerleithen 3
Gala 3 Melrose 0
Hawick 6 St George Edinburgh 0

Semi-Final
Hawick 3 Gala 0
Gala Thistle 3 Hawick and Wilton 0

Final
Hawick 3 Gala Thistle 0

1888

First Round
Gala 10 Jedforest 0
Melrose 3 Hawick 0
Kelso 3 St Cuthberts Hawick 0
Hawick and Wilton 8 Gala Thistle 0

Semi-Final
Gala 3 Melrose 0
Hawick and Wilton 8 Kelso 0

Final
Hawick and Wilton 8 Gala 3

1889

First Round
Hawick 3 Jedforest 0
Hawick and Wilton 3 St Cuthberts Hawick 0
Melrose 3 Gala 0

Semi-Final
Hawick 8 Gala Thistle 0
Melrose 5 Hawick and Wilton 3

Final
Melrose 5 Hawick 0

1890

First Round
Gala Wanderers 9 Kelso 0
Gala 18 Jedforest 0
Melrose 6 Ladhope 0
Hawick Greens 3 St Cuthberts Hawick 0

Semi-Final
Gala 11 Gala Wanderers 0
Hawick 3 Melrose 0

Final
Gala 16 Hawick 0

1891

First Round
Jedforest 6 Duns 3
Hawick 13 Watsonians 0

Second Round
Selkirk Union 3 Gala Wanderers 0
Gala 15 Ladhope 0
Hawick 3 Jedforest 0

Semi-Final
Gala v. Selkirk Union (Selkirk Union scratched)
Hawick 3 Melrose 0

Final
Gala 5 Hawick 3

1892

First Round
Gala Wanderers 3 Melrose 0
Hawick 5 Gala 0
Jedforest 18 Kelso 0
Hawick Athletic 8 Heriots 0

Semi-Final
Hawick 10 Gala Wanderers 0
Jedforest 11 Hawick Athletic 0

Final
Hawick 3 Jedforest 0

1893

First Round
Jedforest 6 Melrose 3
Gala Rovers 3 Gala B 0
Hawick Teviotdale Union 8 Melrose B 0
Hawick 3 Gala 0

Semi-Final
Jedforest 8 Gala Rovers 0
Hawick 16 Hawick Teviotdale Union 0

Final
Hawick 13 Jedforest 6

1894

First Round
Gala 9 Melrose 0
Melrose B 4 Gala Water 2
Jedforest B 2 Hawick B 0
Hawick 2 Jedforest 0

Semi-Final
Gala 10 Melrose B 0
Hawick 10 Jedforest B 4

Final
Hawick 4 Gala 2

*City slickers –
Edinburgh
Wanderers, 1973*

1895

First Round
Hawick 6 Gala 0
Jedforest 18 Gala Water 0
Gala Hearts 5 Melrose 3
Selkirk Union 9 Melrose B 5

Semi-Final
Hawick 8 Jedforest 0
Gala Hearts 3 Selkirk 0

Final
Hawick 11 Gala Hearts 5

1896

First Round
Melrose 6 Gala 3
Hawick 3 Jedforest 0
Selkirk 8 St George 0
Heriots 3 Watsonians 0

Semi-Final
Melrose 3 Selkirk 0
Hawick 5 Heriots 0

Final
Hawick 8 Melrose 0

1897

First Round
Hawick 23 Heriots 0
Gala 3 Jedforest 0
Melrose 8 Gala Abbotsford 5
Selkirk v. Watsonians – Selkirk wo

Semi-Final
Hawick 12 Gala 0
Selkirk 5 Melrose 0

Final
Hawick 16 Selkirk 3

1898

First Round
Hawick 14 Melrose B 0
Melrose 11 St George 3
Jedforest 13 Stewarts 3
Gala 14 Selkirk 3

Semi-Final
Hawick 10 Jedforest 3
Gala 9 Melrose 0

Final
Hawick 12 Gala 0

1899

First Round
Jedforest 11 Melrose 0
Hawick 3 Kelso 0
Edinburgh Athenians 11 St George 0
Gala 6 Selkirk 0

Semi-Final
Jedforest 11 Hawick 0
Gala 3 Edinburgh Athenians 0

Final
Jedforest 3 Gala 0

1900

First Round
Jedforest 21 Institution 0
Melrose 11 St George 0
Gala 3 Selkirk 0
Hawick 3 Edinburgh Athenians 0

Semi-Final
Melrose 6 Jedforest 0
Hawick 3 Gala 0

Final
Hawick 14 Melrose 0

1901

First Round
Hawick 3 Brunstane 0
Kelso 3 Edinburgh Borderers 0
Gala 8 Jedforest 6
Edinburgh Athenians 8 Melrose 0

Semi-Final
Hawick 8 Kelso 0
Gala 8 Edinburgh Athenians 0

Final

Hawick 6 Gala 3

1902

First Round
Melrose A 9 Melrose B 3
Hawick 5 Edinburgh Athenians 3
Gala 11 Watsonians 5
Jedforest 8 Kelso 0

Semi-Final
Hawick 5 Melrose 0
Jedforest 3 Gala 0

Final
Jedforest 3 Hawick 0

1903

First Round
Watsonians 5 Melrose 0
Hawick 15 Athenian Scratch 0
Gala 13 Edinburgh Rangers 0
Jedforest 8 Abbotsford 0

Semi-Final
Watsonians 3 Hawick 0
Gala 5 Jedforest 3

Final
Gala 11 Watsonians 0

1904

First Round
Hawick 3 Edinburgh University 0
Watsonians 5 Morningside 3
Melrose 6 Edinburgh Athenians 3
Jedforest 3 Gala 0

Semi-Final
Hawick 5 Watsonians 0
Jedforest 10 Melrose 5

Final
Jedforest 6 Hawick 0

1905

First Round
Jedforest 8 Hawick 5
Watsonians 10 Melrose 0
Edinburgh Athenians 13 Heriots 0
Gala 13 Corinthians 0

Semi-Final
Watsonians 8 Jedforest 0
Gala 5 Edinburgh Athenians 3

Final
Watsonians 3 Gala 0

1906

First Round
Gala 13 Jedforest 3
Watsonians 11 Melrose 0
Hawick 6 Institution 0
Melrose B 5 Royal High School 3

Semi-Final
Watsonians 17 Gala 0
Hawick 6 Melrose B 0

Final
Watsonians 5 Hawick 0

1907

First Round
Hawick 3 Heriots 0
Watsonians 7 Gala 0
Melrose 10 Institution 0
Clydesdale 3 Jedforest 0

Semi-Final
Watsonians 3 Hawick 0
Clydesdale 8 Melrose 3

Final
Watsonians 13 Clydesdale 0

1908

First Round
Gala 18 Langholm 0
Melrose 3 Jedforest 0
Watsonians 6 Heriots 0
Hawick 6 Royal High School 5

Semi-Final
Melrose 7 Gala 0
Hawick 3 Watsonians 0

Final
Hawick 3 Melrose 0

1909

First Round
Langholm 6 Heriots 0
Gala 3 Royal High School 0
Jedforest 11 Melrose 3
Hawick 9 Watsonians 3

Semi-Final
Gala 8 Langholm 3
Hawick 6 Jedforest 0

Final
Hawick 6 Gala 3

1910

First Round
Gala 3 Langholm 0
Royal High School 11 Melrose 3
Hawick 5 Jedforest 0
Heriots 10 Selkirk 0

Semi-Final
Royal High School 8 Gala 5
Hawick 3 Heriots 0

Final
Hawick 8 Royal High School 0

1911

First round
Hawick 11 Selkirk 0
Gala 8 Royal High School 3
Heriots 8 Melrose 3
Jedforest 6 Langholm 0

Semi-Final
Hawick 13 Gala 0
Heriots 11 Jedforest 0

Final
Hawick 18 Heriots 6

1912

First Round
Heriots 18 Melrose B 0
Jedforest 6 Selkirk 0
Melrose 6 Royal High School 0
Gala 5 Edinburgh University 3
Hawick 13 Stewarts 0

Second Round
Heriots 6 Jedforest 0
Gala 13 Langholm 0

Semi-Final
Hawick 18 Melrose 6
Gala 8 Heriots 3

Final
Hawick 12 Gala 5

1913

First Round
Kelso 8 Melrose 5
Hawick 8 Heriots 5
Walkerburn 5 Langholm 0
Stewarts 11 Royal High School 3

Second Round
Kelso 8 Selkirk 0
Hawick 8 Edinburgh University 5
Walkerburn 3 Jedforest 0
Stewarts 6 Gala 3

Semi-Final
Hawick 5 Kelso 0
Stewarts 8 Walkerburn 5

Final
Hawick 14 Stewarts 0

1914

First Round
Kelso 6 Melrose 5
Stewarts 10 Walkerburn 0
Edinburgh University 5 Langholm 0
Heriots 3 Selkirk 0
Watsonians 10 Gala 0
Edinburgh Wanderers 6 Jedforest 0

Second Round
Hawick 3 Royal High School 0
Edinburgh University 11 Kelso 8
Heriots 3 Stewarts 0
Watsonians 6 Edinburgh Wanderers 3

Semi-Final
Hawick 8 Edinburgh University 3
Watsonians 6 Heriots 0

Final
Watsonians 8 Hawick 0

1915
(*The Khaki Sevens*)

First Round
2/5th Royal Scots 14 Forth RGA 5
Lothian and Borders Horse B 0
    1/4th KOSB B 6
2/4th KOSB 0 Lothian and Borders A 8
1/4th KOSB 6 Royal Scots 0

Semi-Final
2/5th Royal Scots 5 1/4th KOSB B 3
Lothian and Borders Horse A 5
    1/4th KOSB A 0

Final
Lothian and Borders Horse A 16
    2/5th Royal Scots 3

1919

First Round
Royal High School 6 Heriots 0
Hawick 6 Kelso 0

Second Round
Jedforest 3 Gala 0
Melrose 6 Selkirk 0
Stewarts 10 Langholm 0
Hawick 11 Royal High School 8

Semi-Final
Jedforest 13 Melrose 0
Hawick 13 Stewarts 8

Final
Hawick 8 Jedforest 0

1920

First Round
Stewarts 5 Selkirk 3
Kelso 3 Heriots 0
Langholm 3 Earlston 0
Gala 3 Melrose 0

Second Round
Jedforest 6 Edinburgh Wanderers 3
Hawick 3 Royal High School 0
Stewarts 6 Kelso 5
Gala 8 Langholm 0

Semi-Final
Hawick 6 Jedforest 0
Stewarts 13 Gala 0

Final
Stewarts 3 Hawick 0

1921

First Round
Stewarts 3 Watsonians 0
Heriots 11 Edinburgh Wanderers 0
Royal High School 9 Selkirk 0
Melrose 3 Gala 0

Second Round
Kelso 16 Langholm 5
Jedforest 5 Hawick 0
Heriots 3 Stewarts 0
Royal High School 5 Melrose 0

Semi-Final
Kelso 8 Jedforest 5
Royal High School 5 Heriots 0

Final
Royal High School 17 Kelso 5

1922

First Round
Jedforest 6 Edinburgh Borderers 0
Melrose 9 Kelso 6
Heriots 10 Selkirk 8
Gala 13 Edinburgh Wanderers 10

Second Round
Hawick 9 Stewarts 3
Royal High School 11 Langholm 0
Melrose 10 Jedforest 0
Gala 5 Heriots 3

Semi-Final
Hawick 5 Royal High School 0
Melrose 6 Gala 5

Final
Hawick 3 Melrose 0

1923

First Round
Hawick 13 Royal High School 3
Jedforest 6 Selkirk 3
Gala 12 Kelso 0
Watsonians 8 Melrose 3

Second Round
Edinburgh Institution 6 Langholm 0
Heriots 8 Edinburgh Wanderers 0
Jedforest 3 Hawick 0
Gala 3 Watsonians 0

Semi-Final
Heriots 10 Edinburgh Institution 0
Gala 12 Jedforest 0

Final
Heriots 8 Gala 6

1924

First Round
Stewarts 11 Edinburgh Institution 3
Jedforest 10 Heriots 0
Kelso 9 Langholm 5
Royal High School 6 Walkerburn 3
Edinburgh Academicals 3 Melrose 0

Second Round
Hawick 13 Gala 3
Stewarts 10 Kelso 0
Jedforest 9 Royal High School 0
Selkirk 9 Edinburgh Academicals 0

Semi-Final
Hawick 6 Stewarts 3
Jedforest 3 Selkirk 0

Final
Hawick 8 Jedforest 6

1925

First Round
Selkirk 5 Edinburgh Institution 3
Walkerburn 8 Royal High School 0
Gala 6 Jedforest 0
Hawick 13 Langholm 0
Stewarts 9 Melrose B 3
Heriots 14 Edinburgh Academicals 3

Second Round
Kelso 13 Melrose 5
Hawick 3 Selkirk 0
Gala 12 Walkerburn 0
Heriots 6 Stewarts 3

Semi-Final
Hawick 6 Kelso 0
Heriots 14 Gala 13

Final
Hawick 14 Heriots 3

*Boroughmuir –
winners, 1976*

1926

First Round
Gala 16 Edinburgh Wanderers 5
Kelso 11 Jedforest 0
Hawick 5 Stewarts 3
Royal High School 16 Langholm 13
Heriots 8 Edinburgh Academicals 3
Selkirk 6 Edinburgh Institution 3

Second Round
Watsonians 11 Melrose 5
Kelso 8 Gala 3
Hawick 18 Royal High School 5
Selkirk 10 Heriots 3

Semi-Final
Watsonians 11 Kelso 8
Hawick 6 Selkirk 0

Final
Watsonians 8 Hawick 3

1927

First Round
Melrose 13 Royal High School 3
Stewarts 9 Edinburgh Institution 6
Kelso 8 Selkirk 0
Gala 8 Edinburgh Wanderers 0
Hawick 10 Heriots 8
Watsonians 16 Jedforest 5

Second Round
Stewarts 11 Melrose 8
Gala 9 Kelso 3
Hawick 14 Watsonians 0
Edinburgh Academicals 26 Langholm 0

Semi-Final
Stewarts 6 Gala 5
Hawick 6 Edinburgh Academicals 3

Final
Hawick 13 Stewarts 5

1928

First Round
Melrose 13 Selkirk 0
Langholm 8 Jedforest 3
Heriots 6 Gala 5
Edinburgh Academicals 13 Royal High 0
Hawick 11 Edinburgh Institution 0
Watsonians 8 Edinburgh Wanderers 0

Second Round
Melrose 6 Langholm 3
Edinburgh Academicals 11 Heriots 5
Hawick 6 Watsonians 5
Kelso 8 Stewarts 0

Semi-Final
Edinburgh Academicals 8 Melrose 3
Kelso 5 Hawick 0

Final
Edinburgh Academicals 3 Kelso 0

1929

First Round
Stewarts 3 Kelso 0
Royal High School 6 Jedforest 0
Hawick 8 Edinburgh Academicals 6
Melrose 14 Langholm 3
Gala 10 Watsonians 3
Heriots 12 Edinburgh Wanderers 0

Second Round
Stewarts 8 Royal High School 0
Hawick 3 Melrose 0
Gala 13 Heriots 0
Selkirk 11 Edinburgh Institution 0

Semi-Final
Hawick 10 Stewarts 4
Gala 8 Selkirk 5

Final
Hawick 8 Gala 6

1930

First Round

Royal High School 8 Melrose 5
Gala 9 Edinburgh Institution 0
Jedforest 6 Watsonians 5
Heriots 10 Stewarts 0
Edinburgh Academicals 19 Selkirk 0
Kelso 11 Edinburgh Wanderers 3

Second Round

Gala 15 Royal High School 6
Heriots 13 Jedforest 5
Edinburgh Academicals 13 Kelso 0
Hawick 21 Langholm 0

Semi-Final

Heriots 8 Gala 6
Edinburgh Academicals 13 Hawick 6

Final

Edinburgh Academicals 11 Heriots 3

II Complete List of Results and Finalists 1931–1994

1931

First Round
Melrose 18 Heriots 3
Edinburgh Academicals 11 Kelso 3
Selkirk 6 Royal High School 3
Stewarts 16 Jedforest 3
Gala 14 Langholm 10
Watsonians 6 Edinburgh Institution 3

Second Round
Melrose 11 Edinburgh Academicals 5
Selkirk 9 Stewarts 3
Gala 14 Watsonians 3
Hawick 9 Edinburgh Wanderers 6

Semi-Final
Melrose 8 Selkirk 5
Hawick 13 Gala 0

Final
Melrose 10 Hawick 6

Finalists
Melrose: W.J. Nisbet, A.B. McLaren,
R. Mitchell, F. Mitchell, J.W. Allan,
C. Mitchell, J.S. Crawford
Hawick: A.C. Pinder, R.N.R. Storrie,
A.E. Fiddes, A. Bowie, W.B. Welsh,
J. Beattie, R. Foster

1932

First Round
Kelso 9 Melrose 0
Edinburgh Academicals 10 Selkirk 0
Glasgow and District 8
  Edinburgh Wanderers 3
Barbarians 8 Stewarts 0
Heriots 9 Jedforest 3
Hawick 13 Watsonians 0
Gala 13 Langholm 0
Royal High School 3
  Edinburgh Institution 0

Second Round
Kelso 12 Edinburgh Academicals 0
Barbarians 9 Glasgow and District 0
Hawick 6 Heriots 3
Gala 15 Royal High School 0

Semi-Final
Kelso 3 Barbarians 0
Gala 3 Hawick 0

Final
Gala 6 Kelso 0

Finalists
Gala: F.M. Matheson, G. Wood,
T.G. Aitchison, W.W. Barbour,
J.H. Ferguson, A.H. Polson, R. Thomson
Kelso: R.F. Kennedy, A.G. Cameron,
W.R. Bryce, A.D. Bald, J. Graham,
G. Cottington, J.H.P. Blackadder

1933

First Round

Gala 16   Edinburgh University 0
Hillhead High School 11 Selkirk 6
Edinburgh Academicals 18 Melrose 8
Heriots 8 Royal High School 3
Watsonians 17 Edinburgh Institution 4
Stewarts 11 Jedforest 0
Hawick 6 Kelso 3
Langholm 6 Edinburgh Wanderers 5

Second Round

Gala 10 Hillhead High School 6
Heriots 18 Edinburgh Academicals 10
Watsonians 6 Stewarts 3
Hawick 16 Langholm 0

Semi-Final

Gala 10 Heriots 5
Hawick 8 Watsonians 5

Final

Hawick 15 Gala 0

Finalists

Hawick: A.M. McKie, R.N.R. Storrie,
A.E. Fiddes, G.W. Reid, W.B. Welsh,
J. Beattie, R.W. Barrie
Gala: J.H. Anderson, J.R. Short,
G. Wood, W.W. Barbour,
S.D.M. Mercer, A.H. Polson, G. Gray

1934

First Round

Melrose 13 Jedforest 0
Royal High School 8 Heriots 0
Gala 5 Watsonians 3
Hillhead High School 6 Hawick 3
Edinburgh Academicals 16 Langholm 0
Kelso 11 Edinburgh Institution 3
Edinburgh Wanderers 19 Selkirk 8
Dunfermline 11 Stewarts 0

Second Round

Royal High School 9 Melrose 6
Hillhead High School 13 Gala 3
Kelso 16 Edinburgh Academicals 8
Dunfermline 11 Edinburgh Wanderers 5

Semi-Final

Royal High School 3
   Hillhead High School 0
Kelso 5 Dunfermline 4

Final

Royal High School 20 Kelso 0

Finalists

Royal High School: J. Park,
R.C. Logan, W.D. Emslie, T. Murray,
T.S. Brotherston, T.R. Mitchell, R. Bisset
Kelso: R. Service, R.F. Kennedy,
J. Bennet, T. Chalmers, J. Graham,
G.S. Cottington, J.H.P. Blackadder

1935

First Round

Kelso 6 Melrose 0
Edinburgh Academicals 6
   Edinburgh Institution 3
Watsonians 19 Gala 0
Royal High School 15 Langholm 5
Stewarts 6 Hawick 3
London Scottish 18
   Edinburgh Wanderers 5
Heriots 9 Dunfermline 0
Selkirk 11 Jedforest 6

Second Round

Edinburgh Academicals 14 Kelso 3
Watsonians 8 Royal High School 5
London Scottish 8 Stewarts 0
Heriots 14 Selkirk 0

Semi-Final

Watsonians 11 Edinburgh Academicals 6
London Scottish 14 Heriots 11

Final

Watsonians 16 London Scottish 3

Finalists

Watsonians: E.G.L. Mark, E.C. Hunter,
J.J. Sanderson, W. Anderson,
W.C. Morrison, J.M. Johnstone,
G.B. Hendry
London Scottish: F.A.R. Hunter,
R.W. Dunn, M.C. Lucas, A.H.B. Adair,
D.A. Thom, G.B. Horsburgh,
W.A.H. Druitt

*The French
Barbarians –
winners, 1983*

1936

First Round
London Scottish 10 Heriots 6
Dunfermline 6 Gala 3
Edinburgh Academicals 10 Stewarts 3
Watsonians 19 Langholm 3
Edinburgh Institution 6 Jedforest 3
Royal High School 11 Kelso 5
Edinburgh Wanderers 6 Selkirk 5
Melrose 10 Hawick 3

Second Round
London Scottish 11 Dunfermline 0
Watsonians 11 Edinburgh Academicals 0
Royal High School 8
   Edinburgh Institution 6
Melrose 9 Edinburgh Wanderers 6

Semi-Final
Watsonians 8 London Scottish 5
Melrose 6 Royal High School 5

Final
Watsonians 33 Melrose 0

Finalists
Watsonians: R.H. Dryden,
E.C. Hunter, E.G.L. Mark,
G.W. Anderson, J.M. Johnstone,
G.B. Hendry, W.C. Morrison
Melrose: T. Leithead, J.R. Stewart,
A.T. Stewart, G.M. Dobson, R. Cowe,
J.D.H. Hastie, G.H. Rae

1937

First Round
Hawick 16 Heriots 11
Gala 13 Langholm 3
Edinburgh Institution 13 Jedforest 6
Kelso 10 Dunfermline 8
Stewarts 16 Edinburgh Academicals 0
London Scottish 8 Selkirk 0
Watsonians 3 Edinburgh Wanderers 0
Royal High School 13 Melrose 0

Second Round
Gala 14 Hawick 0
Kelso 10 Edinburgh Institution 0
London Scottish 17 Stewarts 3
Watsonians 16 Royal High School 3

Semi-Final
Gala 11 Kelso 8
London Scottish 10 Watsonians 3

Final
Gala 13 London Scottish 11

Finalists
Gala: R.T.R. Dick, J. Dun, J.S. Lawrie,
T.P. Carruthers, A.B. Tod, G.L. Gray,
A.G. Harpur
London Scottish: L. Park, R.W. Dunn,
H. Lind, A.H.B. Adair, G.B. Horsburgh,
A.W.B. Buchanan, D.A. Thom

1938

First Round
London Scottish 10 Selkirk 3
Melrose 10 Dunfermline 3
Edinburgh Academicals 10
   Edinburgh Wanderers 3
Hawick 8 Royal High School 6
Stewarts 19 Langholm 10
Watsonians 6 Gala 3
Heriots 14 Melville College 3
Kelso 6 Jedforest 3

Second Round
London Scottish 11 Melrose 5
Edinburgh Academicals 16 Hawick 5
Stewarts 6 Watsonians 3
Heriots 16 Kelso 6

Semi-Final
Edinburgh Academicals 18
   London Scottish 8
Heriots 6 Stewarts 0

Final
Heriots 10 Edinburgh Academicals 5

Finalists
Heriots: J.B. Craig, J.H.G. Napier,
T. Gray, W.R.C. Brydon, E.J. Oxley,
C.C. Brown, D.W. Deas
Edinburgh Academicals: R.E. Harvey,
C. Ritchie, G.A.F.R. Gibson, B.R. Todd,
I.C. Henderson, E.A. Wright,
A.G.M. Watt

1939

First Round
Heriots 6 Watsonians 3
London Scottish 8 Melrose 0
Hawick 3 Kelso 0
Langholm 5 Selkirk 0
Dunfermline 10 Melville College 5
Stewarts 8 Royal High School 5
Edinburgh Wanderers 12 Jedforest 6
Edinburgh Academicals 8 Gala 3

Second Round
Heriots 11 London Scottish 3
Hawick 11 Langholm 0
Dunfermline 3 Stewarts 0
Edinburgh Academicals 14
   Edinburgh Wanderers 0

Semi-Final
Heriots 6 Hawick 0
Edinburgh Academicals 18
   Dunfermline 0

Final
Heriots 14 Edinburgh Academicals 5

Finalists
Heriots: J.B. Craig, J.G.H. Napier,
T. Gray, W.R.C. Brydon, C.C. Brown,
E.J. Oxley, D.W. Deas
Edinburgh Academicals: R.E. Harvey,
G.A.F.R. Gibson, A.I.S. Macpherson,
H.A. Wilcox, A.G.M. Watt, G.M. Gallie,
M.D. Kennedy

1940

First Round
Melville College 14 Jedforest 0
Heriots 11 Selkirk 3
Hawick 13 Stewarts 5
Academicals-Wanderers 5 Kelso 0
Gala 12 Royal High School 3
Langholm 5 Melrose 0

Second Round
Heriots 9 Melville College 5
Academicals-Wanderers 8 Hawick 5
Gala 16 Langholm 5
Watsonians 13 Dunfermline 0

Semi-Final
Heriots 13 Academicals-Wanderers 5
Watsonians 16 Gala 0

Final
Heriots 18 Watsonians 3

Finalists
Heriots: I.M. Batts, J.G.H. Napier,
I.E. Cochrane, E.O. Kollien,
T.G. Galloway, D.W. Deas, A.L. Barcroft
Watsonians: R.W. Welsh, E.C. Hunter,
H. Wylie, M.R. Dewar, D.G. Heggie,
R. Whiteford, R.N. Easton

1941

First Round
Hawick 3 Melrose 0
Edinburgh City Police 16 Jedforest 0
Watsonians 8 Langholm 0
Academicals-Wanderers 6 Kelso 3

Second Round
Hawick 6 Heriots 0
Edinburgh City Police 22
   Royal High School 3
Watsonians 5 Stewarts 3
Gala 6 Academicals-Wanderers 0

Semi-Final
Edinburgh City Police 6 Hawick 0
Watsonians 13 Gala 5

Final
Edinburgh City Police 13 Gala 3

Finalists
Edinburgh City Police:
G.H. Caithness, R.W. Gollogly,
A.S.B. McLachlan, S. Hogg, J.H. Orr,
J.S. Beattie, L.G. Stirling
Gala: J.A. Caskey, D.F. Mitchell,
M. Dow, G. Carruthers, T.W. Dawson,
G. Lyall, W. Borthwick

1945

First Round
Watsonians 6 Melrose Co-optimists 5
Gala 14 RAF (Charterhall) 0
Hawick (Comb. Trades) 12 Melrose 0
Kelso 3 Musselburgh 0
Langholm 3 Lasswade 0
Academicals-Wanderers 3
   Royal (Dick) Vet. College 0
Hawick Borderers 7
   Combined Services 3
Heriots 6 Royal Navy 3

Second Round
Watsonians 8 Gala 3
Kelso 5 Hawick (Comb. Trades) 3
Academicals-Wanderers 6 Langholm 0
Hawick Borderers 6 Heriots 0

Semi-Final
Watsonians 9 Kelso 5
Hawick Borderers 3
   Academicals-Wanderers 0

Final
Watsonians 6 Hawick Borderers 0

Finalists
Watsonians: J.R. Croxford,
I.D. Robertson, I.J.M. Lumsden,
W. Hamilton, R. Fleming, A.T. Fisher,
G. Kennedy
Hawick Borderers: W.R. Scott,
R. Robson, D. Clark, J. McCreadie,
E. Fairbairn, J.R. Hogg, G. Hook

1946

First Round
Jedforest 8 Gala 6
Stewarts 9 Royal High School 3
Hawick 3 Heriots 0
Watsonians 17
   Academicals-Wanderers 0
Musselburgh 9 Selkirk 3
Melrose 6 Edinburgh City Police 5
Kelso 12 Edinburgh University 0
Langholm 5 Dunfermline 3

Second Round
Stewarts 10 Jedforest 9
Hawick 3 Watsonians 0
Melrose 15 Musselburgh 3
Kelso 9 Langholm 0

Semi-Final
Hawick 6 Stewarts 3
Melrose 8 Kelso 5

Final
Hawick 3 Melrose 0

Finalists
Hawick: W.R. Scott, T. Wright,
J.B. Lumsden, J.R. McCreadie,
D. Valentine, W. Richardson, M. Lynch
Melrose: D. McCulloch, A.R. Frater,
D.M. Hogg, G.M. Dobson, J. Cassie,
H. Stuart, A. Crawford

Eric Paxton and John Jeffrey, 1984: 'Gie me the ba', JJ – it's only 70 yards tae the line!'

1947

First Round
Gala 6 Musselburgh 3
Heriots 8 Glasgow High School 0
Stewarts 8 Langholm 0
Royal High School 5 Dunfermline 0
Kelso 3 Hawick 0
Jedforest 9 Academicals-Wanderers 6
Selkirk 10 Melville College 3
Melrose 13 Watsonians 3

Second Round
Heriots 6 Gala 3
Stewarts 11 Royal High School 3
Kelso 14 Jedforest 3
Melrose 6 Selkirk 3

Semi-Final
Stewarts 14 Heriots 0
Melrose 5 Kelso 0

Final
Melrose 11 Stewarts 8

Finalists
Melrose: T. Hook, A.R. Frater, D.M. Hogg, J. Simpson, A.S. Crawford, H. Stuart, J.W.F. Cassie
Stewarts: A.E. Bennett, J.K. Tait, J.W.C. Foubister, E. Anderson, J. Craig, A.D. Govan, S.G.C. Govan

1948

First Round
Heriots 8 Edinburgh University 3
Watsonians 8 Hawick 0
Kelso 10 Royal High School 0
Stewarts 16 Melville College 0
Selkirk 3 Langholm 0
Gala 6 Edinburgh Academicals 0
Melrose 13 Jedforest 3
Edinburgh Wanderers 11 Dunfermline 8

Second Round
Heriots 11 Watsonians 4
Kelso 6 Stewarts 0
Gala 9 Selkirk 3
Melrose 8 Edinburgh Wanderers 3

Semi-Final
Kelso 5 Heriots 0
Melrose 13 Gala 8

Final
Melrose 11 Kelso 8

Finalists
Melrose: W. Rankin, A.R. Frater,
D.M. Hogg, J. Simpson, W. Anderson,
J.W.F. Cassie, H. Balson
Kelso: G. Wilson, J.M. Thompson,
A. Ferguson, O. Turnbull, D.M. Welsh,
W.C. Henderson, J. Ferguson

1949

First Round
Hawick 11 Gala 3
Jedforest 11 Melville College 6
Watsonians 11 Dunfermline 0
Stewarts 8 Kelso 6
London Scottish 8 Royal High School 6
Heriots 13 Melrose 3
Edinburgh Wanderers 6 Langholm 0
Edinburgh Academicals 16 Selkirk 6

Second Round
Hawick 6 Jedforest 0
Stewarts 6 Watsonians 3
London Scottish 13 Heriots 5
Edinburgh Academicals 11
    Edinburgh Wanderers 8

Semi-Final
Stewarts 5 Hawick 0
Edinburgh Academicals 11
    London Scottish 3

Final
Edinburgh Academicals 8 Stewarts 5

Finalists
Edinburgh Academicals: M. Walker,
D.A. Sloan, H.G. Hay, H. Wregg,
C. McLay, W.I.D. Elliot, R. Keltie
Stewarts: A.S. McDonald,
P.J. Edington, H.G. McCall, E. Anderson,
A. Lowes, H. Campbell, S.G.C. Govan

1950

First Round

Watsonians 10 Edinburgh Academicals 5
Langholm 6 Royal High School 3
Glasgow High School 5 Selkirk 0
Hawick 3 Melville College 0
Melrose 5 Gala 0
Stewarts 6 Kelso 5
Heriots 6 Jedforest 3
London Scottish 10
    Edinburgh Wanderers 6

Second Round

Watsonians 5 Langholm 3
Hawick 6 Glasgow High School 3
Melrose 8 Stewarts 6
Heriots 20 London Scottish 3

Semi-Final

Watsonians 15 Hawick 8
Melrose 9 Heriots 0

Final

Melrose 6 Watsonians 0

Finalists

Melrose: A.R. Frater,
C.W. Drummond, D.M. Hogg, J. Hogg,
J. Johnston, W. Anderson, J. Keddie
Watsonians: H.W. Lyon, R.G. Baird,
G.T. Ross, R. Fleming, D. Millar,
W.H. Barton, D. Mitchell

1951

First Round

Glasgow High School 10 Kelso 0
Edinburgh Academicals 8 Langholm 3
Hawick 10 Gala 9
Heriots 6 Edinburgh Wanderers 3
Rosslyn Park 16 Selkirk 0
Melrose 8 Jedforest 0
Watsonians 14 Royal High School 3
Stewarts 8 Melville College 0

Second Round

Glasgow High School 10
    Edinburgh Academicals 5
Heriots 11 Hawick 0
Rosslyn Park 8 Melrose 6
Watsonians 9 Stewarts 3

Semi-Final

Heriots 11 Glasgow High School 8
Rosslyn Park 11 Watsonians 0

Final

Rosslyn Park 8 Heriots 5

Finalists

Rosslyn Park: J.V. Smith,
J.M. Riechwald, B. Boobyer, J.H. Burges,
P.D. Young, N.E. Williams, R. Crouch
Heriots: T.S. Brown, (I.G. Murdoch),
W.G. McMillan, J.S.W. Stewart,
J. Richardson, K.R. McMath,
R.N. Tollervey, D.E. Muir

They came, they saw, they conquered – Randwick, 1990

1952

First Round
Glasgow High School 11 Watsonians 8
Royal High School 8 Gala 5
Langholm 11 Melville College 3
Melrose 14 Edinburgh Academicals 0
Edinburgh Wanderers 13 Kelso 0
Heriots 8 Hawick 0
Rosslyn Park 13 Selkirk 10
Stewarts 15 Jedforest 0

Second Round
Royal High School 6
   Glasgow High School 0
Melrose 11 Langholm 8
Heriots 8 Edinburgh Wanderers 0
Stewarts 8 Rosslyn Park 3

Semi-Final
Melrose 15 Royal High School 5
Stewarts 5 Heriots 3

Final
Melrose 8 Stewarts 5

Finalists
Melrose: J.L. Allan, A.R. Frater,
D.M. Hogg, J. Hogg, J. Johnston,
W. Anderson, D.M. Brown
Stewarts: T.G. Weatherstone, C. Ross,
J.W.C. Foubister, E. Anderson,
J.C.M. Sharp, W.K.L. Relph,
M.A. Roberton

1953

First Round
Heriots 8 Langholm 5
Hawick 9 Glasgow High School 3
Kelso 13 Edinburgh Wanderers 3
Jedforest 6 Melville College 0
Royal High School 11 Selkirk 0
Melrose 8 Gala 5
Stewarts 5 Watsonians 0
Wasps 5 Edinburgh Academicals 0

Second Round
Hawick 3 Heriots 0
Kelso 8 Jedforest 5
Melrose 6 Royal High School 3
Stewarts 15 Wasps 10

Semi-Final
Hawick 11 Kelso 5
Melrose 5 Stewarts 3

Final
Hawick 11 Melrose 0

Finalists
Hawick: W.R. Scott, R.G. Charters,
N.G. Davidson, J. Wright, J.J. Hegarty,
H. McLeod, A. Robson
Melrose: J. Lyall, A.R. Frater, J.L. Allan,
(R.W.T. Chisholm), J. Hogg, J. Johnston,
W. Anderson, D.M. Brown

1954

First Round
Edinburgh Wanderers 16 Selkirk 0
Langholm 8 Melville College 3
Jedforest 5 London Scottish 3
Melrose 3 Gala 0
Heriots 9 Stewarts 0
Hawick 15 Royal High School 3
Edinburgh Academicals 8
   Glasgow High School 3
Watsonians 13 Kelso 10

Second Round
Edinburgh Wanderers 11 Langholm 5
Jedforest 3 Melrose 0
Heriots 11 Hawick 0
Watsonians 6 Edinburgh Academicals 3

Semi-Final
Jedforest 8 Edinburgh Wanderers 5
Heriots 13 Watsonians 5

Final
Heriots 13 Jedforest 3

Finalists
Heriots: J.M.K. Weir, W.G. Macmillan,
J.S. Stewart, D.S. Dakers, D.E. Muir,
P.S. Shearer, D.B. Edwards
Jedforest: R. Hunter, A. Bell,
W. Renilson, H.F. Campbell, D. Trotter,
W. Borthwick, G. McDonald

1955

First Round
Edinburgh Wanderers 8 Gala 3
Heriots 13 Edinburgh Academicals 8
Hawick 21 London Scottish 5
Jedforest 8 Melville College 6
Watsonians 10 Boroughmuir 3
Stewarts 8 Royal High School 3
Kelso 20 Langholm 0
Melrose 8 Selkirk 3

Second Round
Heriots 14 Edinburgh Wanderers 3
Hawick 11 Jedforest 0
Stewarts 8 Watsonians 3
Melrose 6 Kelso 3

Semi-Final
Hawick 11 Heriots 8
Melrose 8 Stewarts 5

Final
Hawick 28 Melrose 3

Finalists
Hawick: W.R. Scott, E. Broatch,
R.G. Charters, J.H. Bowie, J.J. Hegarty,
H. Scott, G.R. Hook
Melrose: E. Shillinglaw, J. Todd,
A. Hewit, A. Hastie, D.M. Brown,
R. Allan, L.O. Scott

1956

First Round
Watsonians 6 Melville College 3
Kelso 15 Jedforest 5
Gala 11 Langholm 6
Stewarts 16 Melrose 0
Hawick 11 Edinburgh Academicals 0
Heriots 6 Edinburgh Wanderers 5
Boroughmuir 20 Selkirk 8
Combined Universities 15
    Royal High School 0

Second Round
Watsonians 5 Kelso 3
Stewarts 18 Gala 5
Hawick 13 Heriots 0
Combined Universities 8
    Boroughmuir 3

Semi-Final
Stewarts 18 Watsonians 3
Hawick 8 Combined Universities 6

Final
Stewarts 11 Hawick 9

Finalists
Stewarts: T.G. Weatherstone,
J.W.A. Ireland, G. Sharp,
G.M. Robertson, J.C.M. Sharp,
W.K.L. Relph, J.F. Pryde
Hawick: W.R. Scott, G.D. Stevenson,
R.G. Charters, I. Fraser, J.J. Hegarty,
H.F. McLeod, J.T. Mallin

1957

First Round
Edinburgh Wanderers 16
  Boroughmuir 11
Combined Universities 14 Jedforest 0
Langholm 6 Watsonians 3
Heriots 16 Melville College 3
Gala 11 Royal High School F.P. 8
Stewarts 11 Melrose 9
Edinburgh Academicals 5 Selkirk 3
Hawick 11 Kelso 8

Second Round
Combined Universities 12
  Edinburgh Wanderers 0
Heriots 9 Langholm 5
Stewarts 19 Gala 3
Hawick 23 Edinburgh Academicals 8

Semi-Final
Heriots 18 Combined Universities 3
Stewarts 18 Hawick 6

Final
Heriots 26 Stewarts 10

Finalists
Heriots: J.M.K. Weir, E. McKeating,
K.J.F. Scotland, A. Ramsay, D.W. Syme,
R.M. Tollervey, D.B. Edwards
Stewarts: T.G. Weatherstone,
K.R. Macdonald, G. Sharp,
G.M. Robertson, J.C.M. Sharp, W.K.L.
Relph, J. Macpherson

1958

First Round
Melrose 5 Stewarts 0
Langholm 13 Edinburgh Wanderers 3
Hawick 6 Kelso 0
Edinburgh Academicals 13
  Royal High School 8
Co-optimists 21 Boroughmuir 0
Watsonians 18 Melville College 3
Jedforest 10 Gala 8
Heriots 16 Selkirk 0

Second Round
Langholm 8 Melrose 6
Hawick 13 Edinburgh Academicals 8
Co-optimists 19 Watsonians 0
Heriots 15 Jedforest 5

Semi-Final
Langholm 11 Hawick 6
Heriots 8 Co-optimists 6

Final
Heriots 14 Langholm 0

Finalists
Heriots: J.M.K. Weir, E. McKeating,
K.J.F. Scotland, A. Ramsay, D.W. Syme,
R.M. Tollervey, D.B. Edwards
Langholm: T. Grieve, C. Elliott,
J.M. Maxwell, B. Richardson,
A. Warwick, J. Telford, A. Jeffrey

1959

First Round
Langholm 15 Edinburgh Wanderers 0
Melrose 13 Selkirk 0
Jedforest 3 Melville College 0
Watsonians 16 Boroughmuir 13
Edinburgh Academicals 15
  Glasgow High School 10
Heriots 13 Royal High School 8
Gala 18 Kelso 5
Stewarts 6 Hawick 3

Second Round
Melrose 10 Langholm 8
Watsonians 9 Jedforest 6
Edinburgh Academicals 6 Heriots 5
Gala 15 Stewarts 8

Semi-Final
Melrose 8 Watsonians 3
Gala 9 Edinburgh Academicals 5

Final
Gala 9 Melrose 3

Finalists
Gala: K.L. Grant, T. Rainey,
K.W. Anderson, B. Shillinglaw,
A.A. Carson, T. Scott, D.I. Herbert
Melrose: A.T. Hewat, A. Cassie,
D.M. Lawrie, E. Allan, W. Hart,
J.W. Telfer, D.M. Brown

1960

First Round
Melrose 14 Edinburgh Academicals 5
Edinburgh Wanderers 16 Selkirk 3
Cambridge University 13 Hawick 8
Stewarts 11 Langholm 8
Watsonians 10 Kelso 8
Heriots 13 Royal High School 3
Glasgow High School 10
  Melville College 3
Gala 12 Jedforest 0

Second Round
Melrose 14 Edinburgh Wanderers 3
Cambridge University 18 Stewarts 8
Heriots 13 Watsonians 8
Glasgow High School 16 Gala 0

Semi-Final
Cambridge University 20 Melrose 14
Heriots 21 Glasgow High School 5

Final
Cambridge University 28 Heriots 9

Finalists
Cambridge University:
R.H. Thomson, A. Godson,
K.J.F. Scotland, G.H. Waddell, J.C. Brash,
A.W.C. Boyle, M.K. Wetson
Heriots: J.M.K. Weir, E. McKeating,
R.J. Scotland, D. Syme, R.M. Tollervey,
N. Rushbrook, R. Loddard

1961

First Round
Heriots 9 Glasgow High School 5
Kelso 8 Langholm 6
Stewarts 25 Melville College 0
Cambridge University 24 Jedforest 8
Hawick 18 Selkirk 0
Melrose 14 Edinburgh Academicals 3
Edinburgh Wanderers 13 Watsonians 0
Royal High School 16 Gala 3

Second Round
Heriots 11 Kelso 5
Cambridge University 13 Stewarts 8
Melrose 13 Hawick 10

Andrew Ker and Eric Paxton, 1990

Royal High School 15
 Edinburgh Wanderers 0

Semi-Final
Heriots 6 Cambridge University 5
Royal High School 12 Melrose 0

Final
Royal High School 12 Heriots 10

Finalists
Royal High School: J.B. Lacey, J. Blake, D.W. McConnell, J.A. Nichol, J.P. Fisher, E.J. Ireland, G.R.A. Livingstone
Heriots: J.N.K. Weir, E. McKeating, R.J. Scotland, A. Ramsay, D.B. Edwards, R.M. Tollervey, H.M. Mabon

1962

First Round
Jedforest 5 Selkirk 0
Royal High School 6 Kelso 3
Watsonians 16 Glasgow High School 13
London Scottish 11 Heriots 5
Langholm 10 Melville College 5
Gala 11 Melrose 6
Hawick 18 Stewarts 8
Edinburgh Wanderers 6
    Edinburgh Academicals 3

Second Round
Royal High School 28 Jedforest 0
London Scottish 21 Watsonians 8
Gala 8 Langholm 6
Hawick 13 Edinburgh Wanderers 0

Semi-Final
London Scottish 14 Royal High School 8
Hawick 19 Gala 0

Final
London Scottish 15 Hawick 11

Finalists
London Scottish: R.H. Thomson,
J.A.P. Shackleton, I.H.P. Laughland,
J.A.T. Rodd, A.C.W. Boyle, R.I. Marshall,
W.R. Watherston
Hawick: D. Jackson, G.D. Stevenson,
A.R. Broatch, R.G. Turnbull, D. Grant,
R. Valentine, G.H. Willison

1963

First Round
London Scottish 10 Kelso 6
Edinburgh Academicals 9 Melrose 6
Hawick 27 Jedforest 0
Gala 10 Royal High School 6
Boroughmuir 9 Glasgow Academicals 0
Watsonians 20 Selkirk 3
Stewarts 9 Melville College 5
Langholm 8 Heriots 3

Second Round
London Scottish 13
    Edinburgh Academicals 3
Hawick 11 Gala 0
Boroughmuir 11 Watsonians 0
Stewarts 6 Langholm 3

Semi-Final
Hawick 11 London Scottish 8
Boroughmuir 8 Stewarts 5

Final
Boroughmuir 13 Hawick 3

Finalists
Boroughmuir: T.A. Irving, A.D. Leitch,
W. Herries, J.R. Irvine, K.I. Ross,
A. Haggart, J.D. Robertson
Hawick: B. King, E.W. Broatch,
G.D. Stevenson, R.G. Turnbull,
T.O. Grant, H.F. MacLeod, D. Grant

1964

First Round
Melrose 11 Heriots 0
London Scottish 15
  Edinburgh Wanderers 3
Watsonians 16 Jedforest 0
Hawick 8 Kelso 5
Selkirk 8 Melville College 6
Stewarts 11 Langholm 8
Boroughmuir 6 Royal High School 5
Gala 13 Edinburgh Academicals 12

Second Round
London Scottish 5 Melrose 3
Watsonians 10 Hawick 5
Stewarts 23 Selkirk 10
Gala 18 Boroughmuir 5

Semi-Final
London Scottish 6 Watsonians 3
Gala 16 Stewarts 8

Final
Gala 14 London Scottish 8

Finalists
Gala: W.K. Brydon, A.S. Amos,
J.W.C. Turner, D.S. Paterson, J. Gray,
R.M. Paterson, A.A. Carson
London Scottish: D.A. Hamilton,
J.A.P. Shackleton, W.G. McDonald,
J.A.T. Rodd, A.C.W. Boyle,
D.B. Hayburn, W.R. Watherston

1965

First Round
Jedforest 11 Melville College 8
London Scottish 11
  Edinburgh Academicals 0
Gala 18 Heriots 6
Stewarts 8 Edinburgh Wanderers 0
Kelso 6 Langholm 5
Barbarians 16 Melrose 8
Watsonians 18 Selkirk 8
Hawick 15 Royal High School 11

Second Round
London Scottish 16 Jedforest 0
Stewarts 15 Gala 3
Kelso 16 Barbarians 5
Hawick 16 Watsonians 5

Semi-Final
London Scottish 11 Stewarts 10
Hawick 11 Kelso 0

Final
London Scottish 16 Hawick 10

Finalists
London Scottish: C.G. Hodgson,
J.A.P. Shackleton, I.H.P. Laughland,
J.A.T. Rodd, J.P. Fisher, J.G.R. Percival,
J.C. Brash
Hawick: D. Jackson, G.D. Stevenson,
D. Cranston, H. Whitaker, D. Grant,
P. Robertson, N. Suddon

*Bay of Plenty –
winners, 1992*

1966

First Round
Kelso 14 Royal High School 6
Hawick 31 Jedforest 0
Stewarts 9 Selkirk 5
Gala 13 Loughborough Colleges 8
Melrose 19 Edinburgh Academicals 0
Watsonians 11 Edinburgh Wanderers 8
Melville College 14 Heriots 5
London Scottish 16 Langholm 3

Second Round
Hawick 3 Kelso 0
Gala 9 Stewarts 0
Melrose 13 Watsonians 10
London Scottish 8 Melville College 5

Semi-Final
Hawick 18 Gala 0
Melrose 11 London Scottish 10

Final
Hawick 25 Melrose 6

Finalists
Hawick: J. Auchinleck, R.B. Welsh,
C.M. Telfer, H. Whitaker, A. Graham,
P. Robertson, R.W. Brydon
Melrose: R. Blacklock, G.D. Tweedie,
D.W. Chisholm, A.J. Hastie, J. Blacklock,
M. Laidlaw, T.D. Wight

1967

First Round
Langholm 10 Melville College 8
London Scottish 13 Heriots 0
Royal High School 17 Selkirk 3
Hawick 24 Jedforest 0
Kelso 14 Edinburgh Academicals 0
Loughborough Colleges 9 Gala 8
Melrose 12 Watsonians 0
Edinburgh Wanderers 6 Stewarts 0

Second Round
London Scottish 5 Langholm 3
Hawick 14 Royal High School 8
Kelso 15 Loughborough Colleges 5
Melrose 9 Edinburgh Wanderers 0

Semi-Final
Hawick 9 London Scottish 3
Kelso 15 Melrose 3

Final
Hawick 19 Kelso 8

Finalists
Hawick: A. Jackson, R.B. Welsh,
C.M. Telfer, H. Whitaker, R.W. Brydon,
P.C. Robertson, N. Suddon
Kelso: D.T. Wood, A. Tait, A.L. Mole,
L.J. Stevenson, I. Scott, R. Thomson,
C.E.B. Stewart

1968

First Round
Edinburgh Academicals 12 Heriots 10
Melrose 14 Gala 8
Royal High School 16 Selkirk 11
London Scottish 18 Watsonians 11
Jedforest 8 Melville College 5
Hawick 22 Kelso 0
Langholm 12 Stewarts 9
Loughborough Colleges 28
    Edinburgh Wanderers 6

Second Round
Melrose 21 Edinburgh Academicals 5
Royal High School 16
    London Scottish 13
Hawick 11 Jedforest 5
Loughborough Colleges 23 Langholm 8

Semi-Final
Royal High School 11 Melrose 8
Loughborough Colleges 16 Hawick 8

Final
Loughborough Colleges 30
    Royal High School 5

Finalists
Loughborough Colleges: K. Fielding,
P. Simmons, A. Robinson, S. Winship,
R.L. Barlow, G.A.C. Sellar, D. Shaw
Royal High School : A.V. Orr,
I.G.M. Cowper, B. Laidlaw, H.H. Penman,
A.D. Forgan, D.G.L. Pickering, J. Dignall

1969

First Round

Melrose 16 Langholm 10
Hawick 10 West of Scotland 5
Royal High School 15 Kelso 3
Loughborough Colleges 9 Watsonians 0
Selkirk 14 Stewarts 11
Gala 16 Edinburgh Wanderers 5
Edinburgh Academicals 11 Jedforest 8
London Scottish 6 Heriots 3

Second Round

Melrose 18 Hawick 0
Loughborough Colleges 17
   Royal High School 10
Gala 16 Selkirk 5
London Scottish 18
   Edinburgh Academicals 6

Semi-Final

Loughborough Colleges 18 Melrose 8
Gala 13 London Scottish 10

Final

Loughborough Colleges 19 Gala 5

Finalists

Loughborough Colleges: D. Cooke,
P. Simmons, A. Robinson, S. Winship,
D. Shaw, L. Barlow, D. Sellar
(L.E. Weston)
Gala: A.D. Gill, J.N.M. Frame,
A.R. Brown, D.S. Paterson, P.C. Brown,
J. Gray, G.K. Oliver

1970

First Round

West of Scotland 31 Jedforest 0
Gala 12 Royal High School 10
Glasgow Academicals 28 Kelso 3
St Luke's College 15
   Edinburgh Wanderers 8
Melrose 9 Langholm 6
Hawick 11 Watsonians 8
Stewarts 13 Heriots 8
Loughborough Colleges 15 Selkirk 5

Second Round

Gala 22 West of Scotland 3
St Luke's College 15
   Glasgow Academicals 8
Hawick 16 Melrose 0
Loughborough Colleges 20 Stewarts 8

Semi-Final

Gala 16 St Luke's College 8
Loughborough Colleges 10 Hawick 6

Final

Gala 28 Loughborough Colleges 3

Finalists

Gala: A.D. Gill, J.N.M. Frame,
A.R. Brown, D.S. Paterson, P.C. Brown,
J.G. Brown, G.K. Oliver
Loughborough Colleges: K.J. Fielding,
D. Diamond, A. Robinson, S. Winship,
D. Sellar, J. Gray, S. Williams

1971

First Round
Heriots 13 Stewarts 10
Loughborough Colleges 14 Kelso 11
Royal High School 11 Jedforest 8
Gala 11 Langholm 5
Hawick 22 Watsonians 0
London Scottish 13 Selkirk 3
Melrose 28 Glasgow Academicals 5
Edinburgh Wanderers 16
    West of Scotland 3

Second Round
Heriots 15 Loughborough Colleges 11
Gala 21 Royal High School 0
Hawick 13 London Scottish 9
Edinburgh Wanderers 8 Melrose 3

Semi-Final
Gala 18 Heriots 14
Hawick 18 Edinburgh Wanderers 13

Final
Gala 25 Hawick 3

Finalists
Gala: K. Hendrie, J.W.C. Turner,
A.R. Brown, D.S. Paterson, P.C. Brown,
J.G. Brown, N.A. MacEwan
Hawick: D. Gray, A.G. Cranston,
J. Renwick, I. Chalmers, R.F. Broatch,
B. Hegarty, K. Douglas

1972

First Round
Langholm 14 Watsonians 4
Loughborough Colleges 28
    West of Scotland 0
Melrose 20 Stewarts 4
Edinburgh Wanderers 26 Heriots 4
Glasgow Academicals 18 Jedforest 14
Kelso 14 Bridgend 10
Hawick 18 Selkirk 0
Gala 25 Royal High School 0

Second Round
Loughborough Colleges 22
    Langholm 12
Edinburgh Wanderers 15 Melrose 4
Glasgow Academicals 8 Kelso 0
Gala 18 Hawick 6

Semi-Final
Edinburgh Wanderers 16
    Loughborough Colleges 0
Gala 32 Glasgow Academicals 0

Final
Gala 28 Edinburgh Wanderers 10

Finalists
Gala: A.D. Gill, J.M.N. Frame,
A. Brown, D. Paterson, P.C. Brown,
J.G. Brown, G.K. Oliver
Edinburgh Wanderers: D. Tweedie,
R. Proudfoot, K.A.R. Brown,
A.J.M. Lawson, D. Anderson, C. Rumble,
J. Cochran

1973

First Round

Heriots 30 Selkirk 4
Edinburgh Wanderers 22
    Glasgow Academicals 10
Kelso 14 Langholm 8
Watsonians 14
    Yorkshire Wanderers 12
West of Scotland 12 Jedforest 10
Gala 16 Melrose 6
Boroughmuir 30 Stewarts 6
Rosslyn Park 32 Hawick 0

Second Round

Edinburgh Wanderers 28 Heriots 6
Kelso 26 Watsonians 0
West of Scotland 19 Gala 0
Rosslyn Park 20 Boroughmuir 8

Semi-Final

Edinburgh Wanderers 22 Kelso 10
Rosslyn Park 18 West of Scotland 6

Final

Edinburgh Wanderers 16
    Rosslyn Park 10

Finalists

Edinburgh Wanderers: S.L. Briggs,
D. Tweedie, R. Proudfoot,
A.J.M. Lawson, D.R. Anderson,
J. Cochrane, D. Sellar (C. Rumble)
Rosslyn Park: D.J. McKay, J.M. Perrins,
P.J. Simmons, L.E. Weston, R.L. Barlow,
J. Pope, D. Starling

1974

First Round

Jedforest 18 West of Scotland 6
Melrose 14 Edinburgh Wanderers 10
Langholm 10 Gala 4
Heriots 10 London Scottish 4
Boroughmuir 4 Selkirk 0
Glasgow High 18 Kelso 6
Hawick 30 Watsonians 12
Stewarts/Melville 26
    Loughborough Colleges 6

Second Round

Jedforest 16 Melrose 0
Heriots 26 Langholm 0
Glasgow High 18 Boroughmuir 12
Stewarts/Melville 20 Hawick 16

Semi-Final

Jedforest 10 Heriots 4
Stewarts/Melville 16 Glasgow High 14

Final

Jedforest 32 Stewarts/Melville 6

Finalists

Jedforest: G.W. Turnbull, D. Hill,
R.J. Laidlaw, R.R. Mason, R. Lindores,
W. Robson, W. Turnbull
Stewarts/Melville: W. Dorran,
I.W. Forsyth, A. Blackwood, D. Morgan,
A. Brewster, R. Colledge, G. Calder

1975

First Round
Gala 14 West of Scotland 8
Selkirk 12 Hawick 6
Jedforest 14 Kelso 6
Public School Wanderers 24
  Glasgow High 0
Heriots 20 Langholm 10
Edinburgh Wanderers 22
  Watsonians 12
Melrose 18 Stewarts/Melville 10
Richmond 14 Boroughmuir 10

Second Round
Gala 28 Selkirk 4
Public School Wanderers 15 Jedforest 6
Edinburgh Wanderers 20 Heriots 16
Melrose 10 Richmond 4

Semi-Final
Gala 29 Public School Wanderers 6
Melrose 14 Edinburgh Wanderers 12

Final
Melrose 22 Gala 14

Finalists
Melrose: R.A. Moffat, K.W. Robertson,
O.R. Wood, J. Henderson, K.W. Dodds,
N. Stewart, J.G. Smith
Gala: A.D. Gill, D. Carruthers,
A.R. Brown, H. Carruthers, G. Dickson,
J.G. Brown, J.N.M. Frame

1976

First Round
Boroughmuir 28 Kelso 4
Gala 16 Richmond 12
Langholm 18 Selkirk 10
Heriots 16 Jedforest 10
Melrose 14 Glasgow High School 10
Hawick 30 Cambridge University 6
Edinburgh Wanderers 16
  Watsonians 10
Stewarts/Melville 24 Kilmarnock 6

Second Round
Boroughmuir 36 Gala 0
Heriots 22 Langholm 6
Melrose 15 Hawick 10
Stewarts/Melville 22
  Edinburgh Wanderers 10

Semi-Final
Boroughmuir 26 Heriots 10
Stewarts/Melville 16 Melrose 12

Final
Boroughmuir 32 Stewarts/Melville 10

Finalists
Boroughmuir: B. Hay, G. Hogg,
D. Wilson, M. Baillie, N. Morrison,
P. Millican, W. Watson
Stewarts/Melville: A.W. Blackwood,
I.W. Forsyth, I. Duguid, D.W. Morgan,
D. Brewster, D.J. Cartwright,
A.K. Brewster

1977

First Round
Edinburgh Wanderers 34 Heriots 4
Loughborough Colleges 10
   Stewarts/Melville 3
Kelso 16 Kilmarnock 14
Gala 24 Watsonians 6
Melrose 10 Boroughmuir 8
Langholm 16 London Scottish 10
Selkirk 26 Glasgow High 0
Hawick 20 Jedforest 6

Second Round
Loughborough Colleges 14
   Edinburgh Wanderers 12
Gala 18 Kelso 10
Melrose 18 Langholm 0
Selkirk 18 Hawick 6

Semi-Final
Gala 32 Loughborough Colleges 10
Melrose 22 Selkirk 0

Final
Gala 30 Melrose 10

Finalists
Gala: D. Carruthers, E. Henderson,
A.R. Brown, D. Millar, R. Cunningham,
J. Brown, J. Berthinussen
Melrose: C. Ruthven, K.W. Robertson,
O.R. Wood, J.C. Wheelans, K. Dodds,
S. Graham, J.G. Smith

1978

First Round
Stewarts/Melville 12 Kilmarnock 6
Hawick 20 Heriots 4
Selkirk 8 Jedforest 6
Gala 21 Melrose 16
Glasgow High 32 West of Scotland 0
Kelso 16 Boroughmuir 10
Langholm 18 Edinburgh Wanderers 0
Richmond 14 Edinburgh Academicals 4

Second Round
Stewarts/Melville 20 Hawick 12
Gala 26 Selkirk 12
Kelso 20 Glasgow High 4
Richmond 14 Langholm 0

Semi-Final
Stewarts/Melville 10 Gala 4
Kelso 26 Richmond 6

Final
Kelso 22 Stewarts/Melville 4

Finalists
Kelso: G.R.T. Baird, E.A.L. Common,
A.B.M. Ker, R.J. Hogarth, J. Hewit, G.J.
Callander, R.E. Paxton
Stewarts/Melville: A.W. Blackwood,
I.W. Forsyth, D. Calder, C.S. Morgan,
W.K. Tyler, H. Calder, D. Brewster
(D. Cartwright)

1979

First Round
Langholm 12 Jedforest 10
Hawick 16 Melrose 12
Kelso 28 Kilmarnock 0
London Scottish 22 Boroughmuir 18
Edinburgh Academicals 10 Selkirk 0
Stewarts/Melville 16 West of Scotland 6
Watsonians 19 Heriots 16
Gala 22 Rosslyn Park 8

Second Round
Hawick 20 Langholm 4
Kelso 14 London Scottish 10
Stewarts/Melville 20
   Edinburgh Academicals 8
Gala 8 Watsonians 4

Semi-Final
Kelso 16 Hawick 8
Stewarts/Melville 22 Gala 4

Final
Stewarts/Melville 22 Kelso 14

Finalists
Stewarts/Melville: A. Scott, I.W. Forsyth,
S.H. Scott, D.W. Morgan, (A.W. Blackwood),
A. Brewster, J. Calder, D. Brewster
Kelso: G.R.T. Baird, R.D. Monaghan, A.B.M.
Ker, R.J. Hogarth, R.E. Paxton, G.J. Callander,
J.A. Hewit

1980

First Round
Boroughmuir 14 Jedforest 4
Kelso 22 Watsonians 10
Gala 30 Langholm 8
London Scottish 16 Gordonians 10
Melrose 14 Heriots 10
Edinburgh Academicals 16
   Stewarts/Melville 12
West of Scotland 14 Selkirk 10
Richmond 20 Hawick 6

Second Round
Kelso 14 Boroughmuir 6
London Scottish 16 Gala 12
Melrose 24 Edinburgh Academicals 4
West of Scotland 12 Richmond 10

Semi-Final
Kelso 20 London Scottish 4
Melrose 28 West of Scotland 8

Final
Kelso 28 Melrose 12

Finalists
Kelso: M.J. Fleming, E.A.L. Common,
A. Ker, R.J. Hogarth, G.J. Callander,
R.E. Paxton, M. Minto, I. Cassie
Melrose: C. Ruthven, K. Robertson,
J. Cockburn, J. Henderson, K. Dodds,
S. Graham, F. Calder

The Heriots team which beat Kelso 40–16 in the 1982 final.

1981

First Round
Gala 16 Watsonians 14
Melrose 22 Jedforest 4
Heriots 18 Langholm 6
Hawick 22 Richmond 8
Gordonians 15 Boroughmuir 14
Kelso 26 West of Scotland 6
Selkirk 22 Edinburgh Academicals 0
London Scottish 26 Stewarts/Melville 8

Second Round
Gala 16 Melrose 12
Hawick 22 Heriots 10
Kelso 24 Gordonians 8
Selkirk 22 London Scottish 14

Semi-Final
Gala 20 Hawick 16
Kelso 28 Selkirk 14

Final
Gala 26 Kelso 10

Finalists
Gala: P. Dods, J. Whitehead, C.W. Gass,
D. Bryson, D. White, A. Bryson,
R.F. Cunningham
Kelso: G.R.T. Baird, G.J. Brown,
A.B.M. Ker, R.J. Hogarth, J.A. Hewit,
G.J. Callander, R.E. Paxton

1982

First Round
Heriots 40 Langholm 6
Hawick 16 Gordonians 4
Melrose 18 Stewarts/Melville 16
Rosslyn Park 12 Selkirk 6
Watsonians 14 West of Scotland 10
Nottingham 28 Boroughmuir 6
Kelso 26 Jedforest 6
Gala 26 Royal High School 4

Second Round
Heriots 22 Hawick 14
Melrose 18 Rosslyn Park 6
Watsonians 18 Nottingham 10
Kelso 14 Gala 12

Semi-Final
Heriots 12 Melrose 6
Kelso 14 Watsonians 10

Final
Heriots 40 Kelso 16

Finalists
Heriots: P. Hewitt, W. Gammell,
N. Marshall, A.J.M. Lawson, A. Dobie,
P. O'Neill, D. Livingstone
Kelso: R.D. Monaghan, G.J. Brown,
A.B.M. Ker, R.J. Hogarth, J.A. Hewit,
G.J. Callander, R.E. Paxton

1983

First Round
Selkirk 22 Gala 12
Royal High School 14 Barbarians 12
Edinburgh Academicals 6 Glasgow
   Academicals 0
Stewarts/Melville 19 Melrose 6
Hawick 22 London Scottish 10
French Barbarians 18 Watsonians 12
Jedforest 16 Boroughmuir 12
Richmond 26 West of Scotland 12

Second Round
Kelso 32 Selkirk 6
Royal High School 10 Tynedale 4
Bangor 15 Edinburgh Academicals 8
Stewarts/Melville 24 Gordonians 4
Heriots 16 Hawick 12
French Barbarians 16 GHK 6
Jedforest 14 South Glam. Inst. 10
Richmond 22 Langholm 12

Quarter Final
Kelso 22 Royal High School 6
Stewarts/Melville 24 Bangor 10
French Barbarians 16 Heriots 10
Richmond 24 Jedforest 6

Semi-Final
Stewarts/Melville 18 Kelso 14
French Barbarians 30 Richmond 6

Final
French Barbarians 28
   Stewarts/Melville 18

Finalists
French Barbarians: S. Blanco,
J.P. Elissalde, J. Luc Joinel, P. Dintrants,
P. Mesny, E. Fourniol, J.P. Lafond
Stewarts/Melville: A. Blackwood,
S. Scott, D. Wyllie, D.W. Morgan,
A. Brewster, D. Brewster, F. Calder

1984

First Round
Selkirk 18 Royal High 4
Kelso 28 Langholm 0
Hawick 32 West of Scotland 4
Boroughmuir 18 French Barbarians 16
Watsonians 18 Heriots 6
Richmond 14 Melrose 8
Glasgow Academicals 14 Gala 10
Stewarts/Melville 10 Jedforest 6

Second Round
Kelso 30 Selkirk 4
Boroughmuir 16 Hawick 10
Watsonians 26 Richmond 4
Stewarts/Melville 10
   Glasgow Academicals 8

Semi-Final
Kelso 38 Boroughmuir 0
Stewarts/Melville 26 Watsonians 12

Final
Kelso 46 Stewarts/Melville 10

Finalists
Kelso: R. Baird, E. Common, A. Ker,
R. Hogarth, E. Paxton, G. Callander,
J. Jeffrey
Stewarts/Melville: M. Lowes,
A. Malloch, C. Morgan, A. Blackwood,
F. Calder, J.H. Calder, J. Calder

1985

First Round
Boroughmuir 16 Watsonians 14
Stewarts/Melville 22 Hawick 12
Heriots 18 Langholm 6
Melrose 22 Bridgend 4
Edinburgh Academicals 14
    Glasgow Academicals 4
Blackheath 28 Ayr 0
Selkirk 16 Jedforest 6
Kelso 20 Gala 12

Second Round
Stewarts/Melville 24 Boroughmuir 6
Heriots 6 Melrose 4
Blackheath 24
    Edinburgh Academicals 12
Kelso 26 Selkirk 4

Semi-Final
Heriots 22 Stewarts/Melville 10
Kelso 18 Blackheath 12

Final
Kelso 40 Heriots 12

Finalists
Kelso: D. Robeson, E. Common, A. Ker,
R. Hogarth, J. Jeffrey, G. Callander,
E. Paxton, M. Minto
Heriots: D. Buglass, S. Dougherty,
N. Marshall, A.J.M. Lawson, S. Hamilton,
J. Bruce, K. Rafferty

1986

First Round
Gala 20 Langholm 6
The Cougars 24 Glasgow Academicals
10
Jedforest 26 Stewarts/Melville 12
Racing Club of France 24
    Edinburgh Academicals 10
Boroughmuir 32 Heriots 12
Kelso 14 Watsonians 6
Hawick 12 Melrose 4
Wasps 26 Selkirk 0

Second Round
The Cougars 24 Gala 10
Racing Club of France 36 Jedforest 12
Kelso 20 Boroughmuir 6
Wasps 28 Hawick 6

Semi-Final
Racing Club of France 18
    The Cougars 10
Kelso 20 Wasps 16

Final
Kelso 22 Racing Club of France 16

Finalists
Kelso: R. Baird, D. Robeson,
E. Common, A. Ker, R. Hogarth,
E. Paxton, G. Callander, J. Jeffrey
Racing Club of France: L. Pardo,
J.P. Genet, C. Mombet, P. Mesnal,
Y. Rousset, G. Martinex, J.B. Lafond

Mud glorious mud.
The victorious Gala
side of 1994

1987

First Round
Heriots 18 Glasgow Academicals 4
Melrose 16 Wasps 14
Edinburgh Academicals 12 Selkirk 4
Kelso 22 Langholm 0
Hawick 12 Boroughmuir 8
Harlequins 24 Stewarts/Melville 6
Jedforest 12 Watsonians 6
The Cougars 12 Gala 10

Second Round
Melrose 14 Heriots 10
Kelso 22 Edinburgh Academicals 0
Harlequins 30 Hawick 0
Jedforest 12 The Cougars 6

Semi-Final
Melrose 16 Kelso 0
Harlequins 10 Jedforest 4

Final
Harlequins 28 Melrose 8

Finalists
Harlequins: A. Harriman, S. Hunter,
M. Ebsworth, J. McColl, R. Glennister,
M. Skinner, A. Woodhouse, D. Thresher
Melrose: E. Weatherly, A. Redburn,
I. Ramsay, D.K. Shiel, A. Dobie, D. Little,
K. McLeish

1988

First Round
Jedforest 38 Glasgow Academicals 10
Melrose 22 Langholm 10
Gala 28 Selkirk 6
Wakefield 13 Hawick 10
Kelso 20 Heriots 4
The Cougars 28
    Edinburgh Academicals 0
Stewarts/Melville 16 Watsonians 8
Public School Wanderers 22
    Boroughmuir 6

Second Round
Jedforest 6 Melrose 4
Wakefield 18 Gala 14
Kelso 14 The Cougars 6
Public School Wanderers 22
    Stewarts/Melville 18

Semi-Final
Jedforest 16 Wakefield 10
Kelso 22 Public School Wanderers 14

Final
Kelso 14 Jedforest 10

Finalists
Kelso: A. Tait, R. Baird, A. Ker,
R. Hogarth, M. Wright, E. Paxton,
M. Minto
Jedforest: H. Hogg, G. McKechnie,
P. Douglas, R. Laidlaw, B. Law, K. Liddle,
R. Lindores

1989

First Round
Hawick 16 Jedforest 12
Kelso 34 Watsonians 0
Gala 16 Melrose 10
Selkirk 12 Hong Kong 0
Ayr 28 Langholm 8
The Cougars 22 Stewarts/Melville 14
Edinburgh Academicals 24 Heriots 6
Loughborough 11 Boroughmuir 4

Second Round
Kelso 16 Hawick 6
Selkirk 16 Gala 6
Ayr 12 The Cougars 6
Loughborough 18
   Edinburgh Academicals 8

Semi-Final
Kelso 24 Selkirk 6
Ayr 16 Loughborough 14

Final
Kelso 28 Ayr 22

Finalists
Kelso: D. Robeson, R. Baird, A. Ker,
R. Hogarth, E. Paxton, C. Millar,
M. Minto
Ayr: D. Stark, P. Manning, C. McGuffie,
R. Gilmour, D. McVey, K. Nicol,
C. McCallum

1990

First Round
Jedforest 20 Stirling County 10
Kelso 26 Gala 0
GHK 12 Langholm 10
Melrose 22 Watsonians 6

Second Round
Hawick 12 Jedforest 6
Stewarts/Melville 14 Racing Club 8
Kelso 24 Selkirk 6
London Scottish 24 Heriots 16
Edinburgh Academicals 28 GHK 4
Randwick 30 Glasgow 0
Melrose 20 Ayr 16
Harlequins 28 Boroughmuir 10

Quarter Final
Hawick 18 Stewarts/Melville 0
Kelso 12 London Scottish 8
Randwick 20 Edinburgh Academicals 6
Melrose 15 Harlequins 12

Semi-Final
Kelso 22 Hawick 4
Randwick 16 Melrose 15

Final
Randwick 26 Kelso 8

Finalists
Randwick: G. Boneham, J. Maxwell,
L. Walker, D. Campese, M. Ella,
A. Nuiquila, M. Cheika, J. Flett,
D. Phillips
Kelso: D. Robeson, S. Wichary, A. Ker,
R. Hogarth, E. Paxton, C. Millar, J. Jeffrey
(P. Dunkley)

1991

First Round
Selkirk 36 Heriots 4
Hawick 18 Stewarts/Melville 12
Kelso 20 Watsonians 0
Glasgow Academicals 30 Ayr 8

Second Round
Selkirk 21 Stirling County 12
Randwick 14 Langholm 4
Hawick 10 Melrose 6
The Irish Wolfhounds 22 GHK 10
Kelso 18 Boroughmuir 14
Jedforest 18 The Cougars 6
Gala 20 Glasgow Academicals 14
Loughborough Students 30
   Edinburgh Academicals 0

Quarter Final
Randwick 20 Selkirk 12
The Irish Wolfhounds 28 Hawick 8
Kelso 14 Jedforest 12
Loughborough Students 22 Gala 18

Semi-Final
The Irish Wolfhounds 16 Randwick 14
Kelso 16 Loughborough Students 10

Final
The Irish Wolfhounds 28 Kelso 12

Finalists
The Irish Wolfhounds: P. O'Hara,
W. Mulcahy, D. McBride, P. Johns,
B. Hanavan, D. Beggy, A. Rolland,
C. Wilkinson, K. Murphy, N. Francis
Kelso: A. Roxburgh, C. Millar, J. Jeffrey,
R. Baird, S. Barton, J. Thomson,
S. Wichary, P. Dunkley, A. Miller,
S. Bennett

1992

First Round
Currie 20 Heriots 10
Hawick 20 Melrose 10
Stewarts/Melville 14 GHK 12
Stirling County 26 Langholm 4

Second Round
Gala 22 Currie 18
Bay of Plenty 20 Watsonians 10
Hawick 26 Selkirk 12
Edinburgh Academicals 36
   The Cougars 4
Stewarts/Melville 26 Boroughmuir 12
The Irish Wolfhounds 28
   Glasgow Academicals 8
Stirling County 18 Ayr 6
Kelso 14 Jedforest 12

Quarter Final
Bay of Plenty 26 Gala 0
Hawick 26 Edinburgh Academicals 6
The Irish Wolfhounds 20
   Stewarts/Melville 18
Kelso 22 Stirling County 18

Semi-Final
Bay of Plenty 28 Hawick 0
Kelso 28 The Irish Wolfhounds 18

Final
Bay of Plenty 19 Kelso 12

Finalists
Bay of Plenty: P. Werahiko, M. Jones,
L. Edwards, P. Fairweather, K. Irihei,
D. Menzies, D. Kaui, J. Tauiwi, P. Woods,
C. Bidois
Kelso: A. Roxburgh, C. Millar,
S. Bennet, I. Fairley, G. Aitchison,
G. Thomson, S. Wichary, N. Heseltine,
A. Millar, P. Dunkley

1993

First Round
GHK 40 Currie 5
Dundee HSFP 24 Langholm 7
Watsonians 24 Stewarts/Melville 0
Selkirk 19 Melrose 14

Second Round
Edinburgh Academicals 34 GHK 12
Co-optimists 31 Stirling County 7
Gala 28 Dundee HSFP 26
Bay of Plenty 33 Hawick 0
Watsonians 17 Heriots 12
Kelso 22 Glasgow Academicals 0
Jedforest 24 Selkirk 14
Boroughmuir 21 Western Province 10

Quarter Final
Co-optimists 26
    Edinburgh Academicals 5
Bay of Plenty 31 Gala 7
Kelso 33 Watsonians 7
Jedforest 21 Boroughmuir 12

Semi-Final
Co-optimists 14 Bay of Plenty 12
Jedforest 31 Kelso 21

Final
Co-optimists 61 Jedforest 0

Finalists
Co-optimists: C. Hogg, I. Corcoran,
G. Weir, D. Millard, M. Appleson,
G.R. Townsend, A. Stanger, A. Nichol,
K. Milligan, D. Turnbull
Jedforest: C. Brown, K. Barrie,
P. Kirkpatrick, G. Armstrong,
P. Douglas, H. Hogg, K. Amos,
D.K. Shiel, N. McIlroy, C. Hynd

1994

First Round
Stirling County 31 Hawick 7
Gala 36 Stewarts/Melville 0
Heriots 15 Currie 7
Boroughmuir 14 Watsonians 12

Second Round
Melrose 28 Stirling County 19
Villager 42 Dundee HSFP 7
Gala 24 Kelso 7
Manly 31 Edinburgh Academicals 12
Heriots 24 GHK 21
Wasps 19 Selkirk 14
Boroughmuir 19 Jedforest 17
Co-optimists 24 Langholm 12

Quarter Final
Melrose 26 Villager 21
Gala 31 Manly 14
Wasps 26 Heriots 10
Co-optimists 14 Boroughmuir 12

Semi-Final
Gala 19 Melrose 5
Wasps 17 Co-optimists 10

Final
Gala 17 Wasps 10

Finalists
Gala: G.R. Townsend, M. Dods,
(M. Moncrieff), J. Maitland,
G. Farquharson, N. Crooks, I. Corcoran,
J. Amos
Wasps: L. Scrase, A. James,
A. Thompson, A. Gomarsall, D. Shaw,
S. Holmes, R. Scaramuzza

III Competition Rules

Each game (except the final tie, which will be played 10 minutes each way) shall last 7½ minutes each way, and if at the end of the second period neither side shall have won, ends shall be changed, and so on every 7½ minutes (in the case of the final, every 10 minutes) until a side score, who shall be declared victors without further play.

Clubs must turn out punctually. If not they will be liable to be disqualified. The Committee reserve the power to make clubs who are on the ground play off their tie, although not in order of the draw. The interval between semi-final and final shall not exceed 15 minutes. The Referee's decision shall be final.

In the event of a player being injured in any tie the Committee of the promoting club shall have powers to permit a replacement from the same club subject to the following conditions;

(1) During any tie one injured player only on each side may be replaced on the advice of the Tournament Medical Officer.

(2) After the conclusion of any tie any injured player may be replaced for the next and subsequent ties on the advice of the Tournament Medical Officer.

(3) No player who has been replaced at any time may play in any future tie in the tournament.

(4) Once any replacement has taken part in any tie he may himself be replaced only in accordance with clauses (1) or (2) of this rule.

(5) Teams requiring the attention of the Tournament Medical Officer should apply to the Senior Call Steward.

The Committee of the club whose team win the Cup are required to give a guarantee for its safe custody and return.

IV Finals 1883–1994

Winners	Runners-up
1883 Melrose I try*	Gala 0*
1884 Gala I try	Melrose 0
1885 Melrose 3 tries	Gala Union 0
1886 Tynedale 2 tries	Melrose 0
1887 Hawick I try	Gala Thistle 0
1888 Hawick & Wilton I goal, I try	Gala I try
1889 Melrose I goal	Hawick 0
1890 Gala 2 goals, 2 tries	Hawick (scratch) 0
1891 Gala I goal	Hawick I try
1892 Hawick I try	Jedforest 0
1893 Hawick 2 goals, I try	Jedforest 2 tries
1894 Hawick 2 tries (4)	Gala I try (2)
1895 Hawick I goal, 2 tries (11)	Gala Hearts I goal (5)
1896 Hawick I goal, I try (8)	Melrose 0
1897 Hawick 2 goals, 2 tries (16)	Selkirk I try (3)
1898 Hawick I goal, I mark goal, I try (12)	Gala 0
1899 Jedforest I try (3)	Gala 0
1900 Hawick I goal, 3 tries (14)	Melrose 0
1901 Hawick 2 tries (6)	Gala I try (3)
1902 Jedforest 3	Hawick 0
1903 Gala 11	Watsonians 0
1904 Jedforest 6	Hawick 0
1905 Watsonians 3	Gala 0
1906 Watsonians 5	Hawick 0
1907 Watsonians 13	Clydesdale 0
1908 Hawick 3	Melrose 0
1909 Hawick 6	Gala 3
1910 Hawick 8	Royal High School 0
1911 Hawick 18	Heriots 6
1912 Hawick 12	Gala 5
1913 Hawick 14	Stewarts 0
1914 Watsonians 8	Hawick 0
1915 Lothian & Borders Horse A 16	2/5 Royal Scots 3
1916	The Khaki Sevens**
1917	
1918	

Year	Winner	Runner-up
1919	Hawick 8	Jedforest 0
1920	Stewarts 3	Hawick 0
1921	Royal High School 17	Kelso 5
1922	Hawick 3	Melrose 0
1923	Heriots 8	Gala 6
1924	Hawick 8	Jedforest 6
1925	Hawick 14	Heriots 5
1926	Watsonians 8	Hawick 3
1927	Hawick 13	Stewarts 5
1928	Edinburgh Academicals 3	Kelso 0
1929	Hawick 8	Gala 6
1930	Edinburgh Academicals 11	Heriots 3
1931	Melrose 10	Hawick 6
1932	Gala 6	Kelso 0
1933	Hawick 15	Gala 0
1934	Royal High School 20	Kelso 0
1935	Watsonians 16	London Scottish 3
1936	Watsonians 33	Melrose 0
1937	Gala 13	London Scottish 11
1938	Heriots 10	Edinburgh Academicals 5
1939	Heriots 14	Edinburgh Academicals 5
1940	Heriots 18	Watsonians 3
1941	Edinburgh City Police 13	Gala 3
1942		
1943		
1944		
1945	Watsonians 6	Hawick Borderers 0
		Charity Sevens**
1946	Hawick 3	Melrose 0
1947	Melrose 11	Stewarts 5
1948	Melrose 11	Kelso 8
1949	Edinburgh Academicals 8	Stewarts 5
1950	Melrose 6	Watsonians 0
1951	Rosslyn Park 8	Heriots 5
1952	Melrose 8	Stewarts 5
1953	Hawick 11	Melrose 0
1954	Heriots 13	Jedforest 3
1955	Hawick 28	Melrose 3
1956	Stewarts 11	Hawick 9
1957	Heriots 26	Stewarts 10
1958	Heriots 14	Langholm 0
1959	Gala 9	Melrose 3
1960	Cambridge University 28	Heriots 9
1961	Royal High School 12	Heriots 10
1962	London Scottish 15	Hawick 11
1963	Boroughmuir 13	Hawick 3
1964	Gala 14	London Scottish 8
1965	London Scottish 16	Hawick 10
1966	Hawick 25	Melrose 6
1967	Hawick 19	Kelso 8
1968	Loughborough Colleges 30	Royal High School 5
1969	Loughborough Colleges 19	Gala 5

Year	Winner		Runner-up	
1970	Gala	28	Loughborough Colleges	3
1971	Gala	25	Hawick	3
1972	Gala	28	Edinburgh Wanderers	10
1973	Edinburgh Wanderers	16	Rosslyn Park	10
1974	Jedforest	32	Stewarts/Melville	6
1975	Melrose	22	Gala	14
1976	Boroughmuir	32	Stewarts/Melville	10
1977	Gala	30	Melrose	10
1978	Kelso	22	Stewarts/Melville	4
1979	Stewarts/Melville	22	Kelso	14
1980	Kelso	28	Melrose	12
1981	Gala	26	Kelso	10
1982	Heriots	40	Kelso	16
1983	French Barbarians	28	Stewarts/Melville	18***
1984	Kelso	46	Stewarts/Melville	10
1985	Kelso	40	Heriots	12
1986	Kelso	22	Racing Club of France	16
1987	Harlequins	28	Melrose	8
1988	Kelso	14	Jedforest	10
1989	Kelso	28	Ayr	22
1990	Randwick	26	Kelso	8****
1991	Irish Wolfhounds	28	Kelso	12****
1992	Bay of Plenty	19	Kelso	12****
1993	Co-optimists	61	Jedforest	0****
1994	Gala	17	Wasps	10****

     * Ladies Cup
    ** Special Cups
  *** Ladies Centenary Cup
**** Sanderson Silver Salver